WORK FROM HOME

30+ Remote Jobs to
Earn Money with Low
Or No Start-Up Costs

2019 edition

By

David D. Taylor

Published simultaneously in Canada.

From the author: I know you probably want to rush to the core of this book but first thing first, all the legal stuffs that most people usually don't read but that are nevertheless important. So, here it is. In substance it says that you should always verify your information and that you should only make informed decisions after consulting a *competent* professional. In all fairness, this is critical to your success. You will find below the full version of the disclaimer that you will want to read before proceeding further. And please do not reproduce or copy this book without authorization. It represents a lot of work. If you want to receive an authorization you can email your request to berylassetsllc@gmail.com.

Disclaimer: This document is designed to provide accurate and authoritative information in regard to the subject matter covered. It is offered with the understanding that the presenters are not engaged in rendering legal, accounting, or other professional service. If legal advice or other expert advice is required, the services of a competent professional should be sought.

Adapted from a Declaration of Principles which was accepted and approved equally by a Committee of the American Bar Association and a Committee of Publishers and Associations.

The information provided herein is stated to be truthful and consistent, in that any liability, in terms of inattention or otherwise, by any usage or abuse of any policies, processes, or directions contained within is the solitary and utter responsibility of the recipient reader. This information has been obtained from sources believed to be reliable. The author made diligent efforts to ensure accuracy, however it is stressed that the information is provided with no guarantee (1) of accuracy, (2) of absence of error or (3) of absence of omission. You should always verify any and all information through your own sources.

Under no circumstances will any legal responsibility or blame be held against the publisher, the author or Beryl Assets LLC (hereafter and together the "presenters") for any reparation, damages, or monetary loss due to the information provided in this book, either directly or indirectly.

The information presented in this book represents only the opinion of the author as of the date of its publication.

Respective authors own all copyrights not held by the publisher.

The information herein is offered for general information purposes solely, and is universal as so. This book does not provide complete information on the subject matter and cannot, as such, be used as a sole source of information. The presentation of the information is without contract or any type of guarantee assurance. No information contained in this book constitutes investment, tax, legal, stock, equity or insurance advice. This book should not be considered either as communicating an invitation to engage in investment activities. You should determine your own investment decisions and strategies based on your own judgment and on your personal and specific financial circumstances. You should also keep in mind that investments can result in a loss and understand that you should always consult a competent professional before taking any investment decision and before putting any funds at risk.

The trademarks that are used are without any consent, and the publication of the trademark is without permission or backing by the trademark owner. All trademarks and brands within this book are for clarifying purposes only and are owned by their respective owners. Beryl Assets LLC and the Author are not associated nor affiliated with any product, vendor or trademark owner mentioned in this book.

Companies mentioned are for example and illustrative purpose only. No company is endorsed or recommended. Just ideas, for you to decide if it's right for you after seeking the assistance of a competent and appropriate professional: lawyer, accountant, financial advisor, mortgage broker or else. The author, the publisher and Beryl Assets LLC do not provide any legal or other professional advice.

With respect to any third-party website or company mentioned in this book the reader is hereby prompted to read and acknowledge their respective terms and conditions before using them. The presenters assume no responsibility whatsoever in connection with their use.

Table of Content

Introduction

At one time the idea of working from the comfort of your home seemed like an impossible dream. But within the past decade, working from home has gone from being unusual to being a normal way for a growing number to earn a living.

With the democratization of the internet and the development of technologies, companies are employing home-based workers at a higher rate than ever before. By using home-based workers, companies can cut back on office costs and other expenses, provide higher employee satisfaction, have a more comprehensive selection of applicants to choose from, and much more.

For home-based employees the advantages are many. You can earn a paycheck without having to commute, save on traditional work expenses like gas, eating out and work clothes. You can sometimes also cut your daycare expenses, if you have any children, and enjoy more family time. This is a win-win work relationship for both parties.

In this book, I will explore with you what you need to know about home-based jobs before you start your job search. People may have preconceived ideas about what it covers and what it's like to work from home. The truth is that it's still a job and that you must take it as such, with the same standards of professionalism. And no, call center operator or low paid jobs are not your sole options. Some of the 30+ jobs mentioned in this book can help you earn as much as $60 per hour. Some of them may require a specific background, but most of them, almost all of them, do not!

Because I have been where you probably are right now, I have included for your convenience a considerable amount of free resource where you can immediately find countless work from home opportunities. This is the core of this book. Whatever your profile is, whatever your background is there is something for you here! Of course, these resources are *up to date* as of the date of this publication.

Use this book as a resource tool to help you find a work at home job that's right for you, whether you are:

A stay-at-home mom or dad,

A student looking for a few hours here and there to pay the bills,

Disabled and cannot commute,

Retired and need some extra money at the end of the month,

Unemployed for some time and fed up with your traditional job search that leads to nothing interesting,

Somebody who is tired of his on-site job and wants out or who wants the flexibility to focus on more personal projects, like traveling or spend more time with the kids, or

Just somebody who wants to work remotely while earning enough to cover your needs, whatever they are.

Again, let's be clear, **this book is *not* about making a few bucks per month.** This book is about giving you more freedom and options in your life.

I really do wish you the best of luck!

David D. Taylor

New York, March 3, 2019

Chapter 1: The Basics of Working from Home

Before you read about the different types of jobs you can do from home, there are some basics facts, often underestimated, that you should understand. Many articles and books on working from home paint a beautiful picture of a work at home life. You may be able to visualize yourself in your flannel pajamas, sipping coffee as the little ones play on the floor nearby. You take a call, helping out a customer – perhaps helping them decide what size of clothes to buy. Then you take a bathroom break and grab a cookie. You support a few more customers. Later that day, you check your mailbox. You've received a confortable paycheck, and you didn't even have to leave your house!

It sounds great, doesn't it? But in reality, this is not how things always work out. The fact is, many work at home jobs that are very demanding. At times, they can also be stressful. Let's take the position of a work at home call center operator for example (this is just an example, there are many other jobs you can do!).

For some call center operator positions, there is a zero-tolerance policy for noise – so much for the kids playing by your feet. In some call operator jobs you will be timed, not only for minutes spent with a customer but also for minutes spent away from your headset – and there goes the bathroom break!

This is not to say work at home jobs can't be great. They can be! Just don't wear rose colored glasses going into it. Recognize that this is a job, a real job – just one that you work at from home. And you are going to face many of the same requirements that you would with a regular job.

Chapter 2:

Work from Home Scams

W ork from home can be a great way to make money. But, there are also a lot of scams out there. In this chapter, I will cover some common ones so that you know what to look out for when conducting your job search. There are many people out there who only want one thing: to take advantage of you. And the tricks used are more sophisticated every day. Be sure to read this chapter carefully.

How to Identify Scams?

Search Legitimate Forums

The easiest way to figure out if a work at home job is a scam or not is to search legitimate forums. Most legitimate positions will be discussed in forums. It is essential that you visit a quality forum. I once posted on a work at home scam forum that in my opinion the jobs offered from a company were not a right way to make a decent income online. My account on the panel was banned because the owners had a business relationship with that company, and they did not want negative reviews. One of my favorite forums is WAHM.com:

http://www.wahm.com/

Google is Your Friend

Many times you can find if a company is a scam by just Googling the name of the company, plus words such as "Company X + scam," or "Company X + rip off," *etc.*

If you have received an email from a company offering you employment, copy and paste a small section of the email with quotes around it in the Google search bar, to see if that brings anything up. Often, scam companies send out hundreds of thousands of emails, and if it is a scam, you will likely be able to find online comments posted by other employees. Now, review them. Don't just read the big titles as they may be misleading. Also, do not review just one comment. It may happen that the person had a bad experience and felt frustrated about it. That happens. Read more reviews and then make your opinion about the company and the job offer.

Just Say NO When Asked to Collect Cash or Cash Checks

One common scam with a lot of twists involves having you cash a check or money order.

In one scenario, you will be asked to collect money for goods or services from a customer, then send the money to a company, who will then send the customer the products and pay you your share. Unfortunately, you don't get paid, and the customer doesn't get his goods.

Another variation of this is done under the guise of mystery shopping sites. You are asked to cash a check or money order and wire back the rest of the money, keeping a generous amount for yourself. By the time the check bounces, the bogus employer has disappeared, and you are required to pay the cash.

Watch Out for the Free Samples

Some unscrupulous people will get away with anything they can, and that includes asking for writing samples and then not paying. In one ruse, the "employer" ask the potential "employee" to sign up for a free dating site and write several sample reviews of the place.

The "employer" would then get an affiliate commission when the unknowing writer signs up for the dating site. They will also disappear with the writing samples and then use them on other sites.

When you are asked for sample work, a customer should be satisfied with looking at work you have done previously. Unfortunately, there are too many people out there willing to rip off others artistic designs, writings, and other work.

Never do work for a customer without getting at least partial payment.

Pay for Work

There are some companies that require you to pay for job leads. Some of these companies are legit, but many are not. You will have to do your own due diligence for each of them.

As a general rule, I would suggest trying to avoid any company that requires an upfront payment for finding you a job. Companies that take a fee *after* you have received the work are different. In this book, I have only listed one website that requires a payment, actually an upfront payment, and that's it. Everything else is free and at most you just have to register in order to use the platform.

Extensive Training

For certain types of online work, you may benefit from taking a course. However, be sure to check out reviews on the company thoroughly, and when possible, discuss with people who have completed the training. Check forums and Google for reviews about the course before committing. Find out how many have successfully gotten jobs after completion. A few years ago, I was working in a shared office space, one of these places where several companies share the space and basically rent a room or a cubicle. I was taking a coffee break in the kitchen when I witnessed a person assaulting another. The noise quickly brought attention and in no time the cops where in the place. It was an "unsatisfied customer" expressing his feelings to a guy running a training program for prospective work from home employees. The problem was that the client referred several family members and friends, all of whom paid money upfront to this program but nobody could find any job. So here, you can find a little bit of everything: the good, but also the ugly. Do your due diligence before paying a dime and start by doing a search online.

Classic Scams

There are some classic scams that have been around for many years. Two of the most popular are envelope stuffing and craft assembly.

With the envelope stuffing scam, you are told that you can make money with every envelope stuffed. Once you have paid for the "system," you receive examples of flyers you are supposed to place around town, inviting others to send you money to learn how to do the same thing.

With the craft assembly scam, you pay for kits to assemble an item and you are told you will be paid for each piece you complete. However, no matter how perfect each one you collect is, it is never good enough for you to get paid.

Unsolicited Emails Offering Work

Did you apply for the job you are considering, or did you get an unwanted email? Be extra careful of unsolicited emails. These are most likely scams.

Get Rich Quick

It is so easy to believe the get the rich quick hype. But working from home requires dedication and hard work. Do not assume anything that tells you otherwise. Do not fall for "get rich quick schemes."

Chapter 3: The Pros of

Working from Home

The benefits of working from home are just many. Nonetheless, we'll briefly go through a few of them. The main advantages include the following:

1. You choose and manage your own schedule

Today, most of the work done remotely is on a flexible schedule. For instance, if you're a content creator or a web developer, you can almost certainly do your writing or coding any time it suits you provided you meet deadlines. Therefore, if you're a night owl, you can rejoice! With this kind of control, you can put in your eight hours without necessarily beginning at 8 in the morning.

Do you like working at specific hours? Well, by working from home, you'll still have time for a personal break to do anything you want. Even if you only have ten minutes, you can do something that wouldn't otherwise be possible (or thinkable) in a traditional office: take a refreshing power nap, bust a couple of samba moves, listen to a few tunes from your favorite radio station, or even play your guitar! You are sure to return to work feeling a lot more refreshed than you would after a few minutes at a desk browsing the internet.

2. You save money

Without a doubt, when you don't need to bear all those commuting costs, you'll see an instant change in your bank account. You'll also see savings in other places; for instance, you will no longer have to force yourself into formal suits and polished shoes if that is indeed not your style. It also means you will no longer have different wardrobes (for your job and the rest of your life) and dry-cleaning expenses. You will also save on food costs because if you work from home, you will be able to whip up your coffee and lunch instead of buying them from a local store.

3. If you have a team, you can have enjoyable and very productive meetings

I bet you can't give me a single name of anyone who likes meetings (even the free coffee and donuts can't beat the dreary, stuffy conference room, and the pen-clicking sales guy). By working remotely, you not only get to choose your breakfast and seat, but you also tend to be a lot more efficient. With just a couple of clicks, you can have fifteen people on a video call that probably lasts ten minutes instead of thirty—and you can use the video call's chat function to share documents quickly (forget creating copies or having everybody search their emails) or in adding all the critical comments without interrupting anyone.

4. You'll have the opportunity to learn more and become more independent

Working from home means you don't have any colleagues a couple of feet away from you or a tech team one floor up. This means you automatically find yourself developing the skill of seeking answers for your tech-related problems and becoming more active in finding what you need all by yourself. While you can still get help or ask questions when you need to, most of the time, you'll see yourself going the extra mile of checking out your company's wiki, doing a Google search, or even downloading a free guide to find your answers.

Moreover, working from home also means you'll end up learning new essential skills because you need them to work contentedly remotely. For instance, you'll probably realize that the development of the ability to write more concise and clear emails, and sensitivity to the different schedules of your team (if you have any) out of necessity.

5. You can fashion an office out of anything and locate it anywhere

Working from home does not mean you have to get some clunky desk that takes up a corner of your living room, an ugly office chair, and a large monitor. How you set up your home office is a personal choice; you can fit your office anywhere it fits your life. One of my friends who is a remote worker conveniently uses his kitchen breakfast bar as a standing desk (imagine all those health benefits and zero investment). One of my other friends fashioned a section of her bedroom closet into some 'hidden' office so that at the end of the day, she just shuts her work away!

In case you're wondering, you're not tied to your home either, and it doesn't mean that the only other option is the coffee shop around the corner. You can comfortably do your job while traveling, having fun in the great outdoors, or even while enjoying your favorite orchestra at a live concert. All you might need is your laptop (or a smartphone) and an active internet connection.

Chapter 4: How to Transition from a Traditional 9-5 On-Site Job to Home-Based Work

It seems that more and more people are kissing all the lifeless cubicles and stuffy work environments goodbye and opting for the freelance lifestyle where they can become their bosses, or just to work remotely and be in control of their schedules and most of their work. *Forbes* reported that today, about a third of workers in the US consider themselves as freelancers. Indeed, a significant shift is happening in the workforce.

If you've been thinking of jumping on the bandwagon yourself, or perhaps you've been longing for that day when you can bid your boss goodbye, walk out, and never look back, you're not alone. However, if that is the case, it means that you are perhaps like most people who although want to become freelancers, there's always something keeping them from actually doing so. That thing is fear and uncertainty.

Without a doubt, strolling out of that secure 9-5 job and rolling the dice as an inexperienced freelancer can indeed be enough to have you quivering in your boots. Nevertheless, as most people have discovered, it's definitely and surely doable. If you're wondering 'how,' there's something you ought to know, something that will help you successfully transition from your regular 9-5 into a freelance life:

1. Don't forget to check your contract

If you can start building your freelance business while still in the comfort of your steady paycheck, that's awesome! Nonetheless, you cannot afford to skip this critical step.

Some companies have stipulations in their employment contracts that essentially prevent their employees from taking on work from outside that could be competitive with their own business in a way. Therefore, before you try growing your side hustle, you should try combing through your contract again to ensure you are not going to ruffle any feathers.

If you have a difficult time trying to wade your way through all the legalities, you can set up an appointment with HR. The important thing here is to be well-informed beforehand.

2. Begin early

Unless you have stacks and stacks of cash stored in your attic, there's no way you're going to be able to make a seamless leap from your present job without any prior planning. Regardless of what your ambitions and dreams, you still need a means by which to pay all your bills and meet all your basic needs.

This means you have to start building your freelance career before jumping ship from your 9-5; you have to create what many would call a side hustle. You can start taking on some projects you can complete over the weekends or after work—this means you should not try working on these during your regular working hours—so that you can start growing a client base and establish your brand as a freelancer early.

As you will realize, this will most likely translate into spending long nights and weekends in front of your computer screen. Cumbersome as it may seem or be, it is worth the effort and is what it'll take to begin building a robust foundation from which you can grow your home-based business.

3. Explore your options and choose the leap

Regardless of how well prepared you are, the truth is that making the final leap from your full-time job to a freelance career can be gruesomely scary. If preparing as we've discussed so far still fails, to take out the fear over the idea of leaping, perhaps it is essential to take a bit more time to explore all the options before you make the jump.

Maybe your current employer will let you take a part-time role. With this working arrangement, you'll still be able to get your paycheck while also having time that you can use to work on your own business; perhaps your employer is the kind type that would love to be your first customer as a freelancer.

If all the above are not viable options: the terms of employment are against you, your employer will hear none of it, and things like that, you can also decide to save enough money first so that when you leave, you can sustain yourself for a given (projected) period.

What I mean is you never really know. You should thus not try to count anything out; ensure you are considering all possibilities. Perhaps it's what will make all the difference in the long run.

Gradually, you will get to a point where you no longer have the time to commit yourself adequately to the regular job and freelance projects. While that can turn out to be stressful, this is a pretty good sign, as it means you have put together up a steady enough foundation and can now transition from your regular job without necessarily having to worry about the sheer panic.

Thus, when you primarily feel ready (even though, fair warning, you may never feel completely prepared to leap), it is now time to make a move and begin your new life as a freelancer or home-based worker. From personal experience, I can tell you that while jumping ship is indeed frightening; it's also amazingly exhilarating!

Don't forget to have fun in the process. You earned it!

4. Network

You probably already have a good understanding of the significance of networking; regardless, now that we're here, I will drive the point home.

When you're just beginning your freelance business, some of your most significant assets will be the people you have in your web of contacts. They might either have some work for you or have the capacity and chance to link you up with other professionals who could gain from your services.

Therefore, you need to get out there as early as possible, attend networking events, seminars, and conferences whenever you can. Join the industry-relevant associations. Set up informational interviews and meetings with businesses and people that interest you. Send tailored LinkedIn notes or even an announcement saying something like "I am freelancing" to a number of your existing contacts. Just place yourself out there; these connections will soon pay dividends as you build your freelance business.

Now that we have the preliminaries out of the way, let's discuss some of the most profitable work-from-home opportunities available to you.

Chapter 5: Remote Employment Opportunities and Freelance Jobs

These jobs, although home-based, require that you trade your time for revenue. These jobs are much like a 9-5 job in that if you stop working, you end earning. The main difference is that instead of commuting to an office, you can complete these jobs from home. Most people start here, as this can help them accumulate enough money to grow a passive income business. Passive income refers to an activity that brings you a continuous stream of income for something that you only do once. This book is only about finding active home-based jobs. If you are also interested in supplementing your active income by a passive one, I would recommend a book by David Berman on the subject ('Passive Income: Simple Ideas to Start Earning a Passive Income Today to Add Some Money in Your Bank Account or to Change Your Life').

Before going into the specifics, I am going to provide you a great list of job boards. You probably know some of them, but this book is aimed at being a reference guide where you can find everything you need in one place. This is going to be our default list, the one that you can refer to whatever job you are looking for. You will find excellent remote job opportunities on these boards by typing the words "remote" or "work from home" with or without a specific job title. If possible, do not enter a location, other than a country, as it will be irrelevant and will limit the number of offers that you will find. Note however that in a number of cases employers will ask you to be located in a specific country, often for employment laws or tax laws purposes. Do not restrict yourself to the country where you live, as long as you meet the requirement of the employer or client.

Our general list

Action Without Borders *(Idealist)*

www.idealist.org

Careerbuilder

www.careerbuilder.com

Craigslist

To search for the entire United States:

www.adhuntr.com

www.searchcraigslist.org

Daily Muse, Inc

www.themuse.com/jobs

Disabled Person, Inc.

www.disabledperson.com

Fiverr

www.fiverr.com

FlexJobs *(Not Free)*

www.flexJobs.com

FreeeUp

www.freeeup.com/become-worker/

Freelancer

www.freelancer.com

Employment Options <u>*(for recipients of SSDI & SSI)*</u>

www.myemploymentoptions.com/job-
openings/

Europe Remotely

(Not just for workers located in Europe)

www.europeremotely.com

Glassdoor

www.glassdoor.com

Guru

www.guru.com

Hired

www.hired.com

Indeed

www.indeed.com

JobisJob, SL

www.jobisjob.com

Jobspresso

www.jobspresso.co

Landing Jobs

www.landing.Jobs

LifeBushido

www.lifebushido.com

LinkedIn

www.linkedin.com (Job section)

Neuvoo

www.neuvoo.ca

NS Virtual Services

www.nsvirtualservices.ca/vas-apply-now/

Outsourcely

www.outsourcely.com/remote-workers

People per Hour

www.peopleperhour.com

Power to Fly

www.powertofly.com/jobs/

Remote OK

www.remoteok.io

Remotive

www.remotive.io

Resume-Library.com

www.resume-library.com

Skip the Drive

www.skipthedrive.com

StartUs

www.startus.cc/jobs/remote-work

Telecommunity's Remote Job Board

www.remotejobs.telecommunity.net/search-job-categories/

Upwork

www.upwork.com

Virtual Vocations

www.virtualvocations.com

Wemote

www.workwemote.com/candidates/home

We Work Remotely

www.weworkremotely.com

Working Nomads

www.workingnomads.co

ZipRecruiter

www.ziprecruiter.com

Zirtual

www.zirtual.com

Now, let's go into the specifics!

I have divided this chapter into 33 sections, one for each job I am going to discuss. In each section you will find specific job boards where you can find great job opportunities in pertaining to each specific industry.

All the references in this book are up to date as of the date of this publication. However, some websites might not have any opening available when conducting your search. That can happen. Just come back later and keep moving to the next website.

You will find more job offers here that you can possibly digest all by yourself.

1. Transcriptionist

This job can pay $25 per hour or even more. I would recommend this job if you're looking for a flexible job that doesn't require any prior experience or very little when it does.

Transcription entails merely you listening to some audio files and typing everything that is being said. Transcriptionists are often used by medical professionals, but there are legal, financial, and other kinds of transcriptionists as well, such as college lectures.

Since the job is relatively easy, companies are hiring transcriptionists that have little or no experience and therefore, you'll find some job postings only asking you to have a computer and an internet connection to begin. Many companies will allow you to create your own schedule.

Common Requirements

Computer: Excellent computer skills.

Word Processing Skills: Above average typing skills with a high level of accuracy.

Knowledge: Knowledge of the terminology for the type of transcription, such as medical or legal terminology.

Training: Certification or training courses may be preferred, or required, by some employers.

Communication Skill: The ability to listen carefully and take direction easily.

Pay: Pay rates vary and may be dependent on speed. On average, those starting out may make around $10, and work their way up to $20+ per hour.

How to Find a Job in This Field?

If you're just getting started, here are some leads on where to find transcription jobs even as a complete beginner:

1888typeitup

www.1888typeitup.com/transcription-jobs

Aberdeen

www.abercap.com/careers/

AccuTran Global

www.accutranglobal.com

Allegis Group

www.allegisgroup.com/en/careers

Bam! Transcription

www.bamtranscription.com

Birch Creek Communications

www.birchcreekcommunications.com

Cambridge Transcriptions

www.ctran.com/employment/

CrowdSurf

www.crowdsurfwork.com

Fast Chart

www.fastchart.com/about/careers/

GMR Transcription

www.gmrtranscription.com

NRG&CO

www.nealrgross.com

nThrive (Adreima)

www.nthrive.com

OpenSpace *(foreign language transcriptionists)*

www.crowdsource.com/workforce/

Quicktate

www.quicktate.com

Rev

www.rev.com

Scribie

www.scribie.com

Tigerfish

www.tigerfish.com

Transcriptions'N Translations

www.tntmiami.com

TranscribeMe!

www.transcribeMe.com

Transcribe Anywhere

www.transcribeAnywhere.com

Ubiqus

www.ubiqus.com

Verbalink

www.verbalink.com

Please note that before someone hires you, most employers will give you a short test to help them measure your attention to details and your typing accuracy before hiring you for any official tasks.

2. Virtual Assistant

Today, many companies are hiring self-employed virtual assistants to save on employment costs. This a catch-all category in a sense. A virtual assistant can be needed to complete a variety of tasks like booking a hotel reservation, conducting online research, managing calendars, replying emails, entering or processing data... It's very broad but usually a virtual assistant will perform basic secretary work for you.

Common Requirements:

Computer: Excellent computer skills.

Word Processing Skills: Accurate data entry and typing skills are needed for many virtual assistant jobs.

Knowledge: Depending on what type of virtual assistant you are, you may need medical, financial, SEO, or other expertise.

Communication Skills: Ability to communicate with the client and take direction.

Organization: You will need to be very organized to work on a variety of tasks and be able to meet deadlines. I would say that this is the perfect job for you if you're extremely organized and great at multitasking.

How Much Can It Pay?

The pay for a virtual assistant varies greatly depending on the client, location, and expertise needed. Rates may be set per hour, per project, or by the month. Usually, you can expect to make anywhere from about $10 to about $30 and sometimes more. Now, realistically, you are more likely to earn around $15 per hour. One important factor to take into account is whether you are going to have expenses. If you set a price per project, by just to incorporate any expenses you might have, like stamps, paper, tuner for the printer and so on. It might not seem like much but it adds up quickly, so do not work at a loss!

How to Find a Job in This Field?

If you're in this type of work, you can scrutinize platforms such as the ones below to find virtual assisting opportunities.

Aspire Lifestyles

www.aspirelifestyles.com/en/careers

Assistant Match

www.assistantmatch.com

Belay, Inc.

www.belaysolutions.com

Cass Information Systems, Inc.

www.cassinfo.com/careers

Clickworker Gmgh

www.clickworker.com/clickworker/

Contemporary Virtual Assistance

www.cva.bamboohr.com/jobs/

DionData Solutions

www.diondatasolutions.net/opportunities.htm

Equivity

www.equivity.recruitee.com

Fancy Hands Inc.

www.fancyhands.com

GabbyVille

www.gabbyville.com

(Email HR at career@gabbyville.com)

HEA-Employment.com

www.hea-employment.com/job/

Insignia SEO

www.insigniaseo.com/careers/

(You must apply through Indeed)

Konsus

www.konsus.com/career

Mturk (Amazon Mechanical Turk)

www.mturk.com/mturk/welcome

OkayRelax LLC

www.okayrelax.com

Paragon Planners

www.paragonplanners.com/opportunities.php

People Per Hour Ltd

www.peopleperhour.com

Red Butler (not free)

www.redbutler.com/careers

Team Delegate, LLC.

www.onerecruit.com

The Appointment Biz.com

www.theappointmentbiz.com

Vicky

www.vickyvirtual.com/join-team/

Virtual Gal Friday, LLC

www.virtualgalfriday.com

Virtual Office Temps

www.virtualassistantjobs.com

Virtual Office VA Staffing

www.virtualofficeva.com/apply-to-be-a-va.html

Worldwide101

www.worldwide101.com

3. Clickworker and Other Short Tasks

A number of websites, called Gig Sites, let you advertise very small services that you are willing to perform. If you can come up with "gigs" that are simple to do, this can be a fast way to make money. For example, you could offer to send a postcard from your area. Take a look at the gigs on this website to get ideas.

Common Requirements

Computer: Ability to post your gigs (services) and respond to those looking for what you are offering.

Social Media Skills: It helps to know how to promote your gigs on sites such as Facebook and Twitter.

Organization: You will need to keep track of the gigs you are offering, who has ordered what, *etc.*

Reliability: You must complete tasks in a timely fashion, or they will expire, and you will not get paid.

How Much Can It Pay?

It depends from one site to another and a website to another. If you take Fiverr.com for instance, a lot of freelancers offer small services starting at $5.

How to Find a Job in This Field?

You can start with the following websites:

Fiverr

www.fiverr.com

Clickworker

www.clickworker.com

Gigbucks

www.gigbucks.com

Microworkers

www.microworkers.com

Mturk (Amazon)

www.mturk.com/mturk/welcome

4. Website Tester

This job can pay about $10 to $15 for every test taken (a test can take 10 to 15 minutes to complete. It's variable).

Many companies are paying online website testers to ensure their websites are intuitive and easy to navigate. As a website tester, you mostly follow the instructions provided to you to check out the site. An average test will take about fifteen minutes. If you choose this option, you should consider registering with up to twelve different companies because the opportunities to test these sites are on a first-come-first-serve basis. In case you're wondering, some freelance website testers earn up to $2,000 per month.

How to Find a Job in This Field?

Start with the sites listed below. Make sure to register with many different companies for chances to test as many websites as you can.

Analysia

www.analysia.com

Applause App Quality, Inc (UTest)

www.utest.com

Mechanical Turk (Amazon)

www.mturk.com

TestingTime AG

www.testingtime.com

TryMyUI

www.trymyui.com

Userfeel Ltd

www.userfeel.com

Userlytics

www.userlytics.com

UserTesting

www.usertesting.com

UserZoom (intellizoom)

www.youeye.com

WhatUsersDo

www.panel.whatusersdo.com/become-a-tester/

ZURB, Inc.

www.enrollapp.com

When you get into the system, you will get emails when companies require testers, and if you are the first one to respond, you should expect to take about 15 to 20 minutes to finish the test. Most sites will need you to have a webcam and a microphone, which you don't need to worry about anyway because they're built into most laptops. Tester sites usually pay through PayPal within one or two weeks.

5. Search Engine Evaluator

Millions of searches are done on the Internet daily. Search engines, such as Bing and Google, use algorithms to give searchers the best results. Work at home search engine evaluators check the results of searches conducted through search engines to make sure they are accurate. They will type a phrase into the search engine and analyze if the results are relevant.

Common Requirements

Computer: High-speed Internet access with anti-virus and anti-spyware software.

Education: A Bachelor's Degree or equivalent is usually preferred.

Excellent Analytical Skills: Ability to analyze search results. You may be required to pass a test before being hired.

Communication Skills: Ability to communicate results accurately and precisely.

Second Language Skills: Some positions will require that you are fluent in another language. You will have to demonstrate this by passing a language assessment test.

How Much Can It Pay?

You can expect to make around $15 per hour as a search engine evaluator.

How to Find a Job in This Field?

You can start your job search with the websites listed in the introduction of this chapter. You can then complete your search with the following websites.

iSoftStone

www.isoftstone.com

Leapforce

www.leapforceathome.com/qrp/public/jobs/list

Lionbridge

www.thesmartcrowd.com/workers/job-opportunities/

Workforce Logiq

www.workforcelogiq.com/join-our-team/

Appen

www.appen.com

6. Call Center Operator

The outlook for work at home call center operators is excellent. More and more companies are using at home teleworkers to increase their productivity, giving them a more abundant source of applicants to select from while helping them to save costs.

As a call center operator, there are a variety of jobs you may be working at. You could be making outbound calls, such as sales calls or research calls, or inbound calls, such as taking orders or providing technical support. Call center operators usually fit into two categories: customer service and sales representative and technical support employee. In both cases the employer will provide the training. However, in some cases, you will be required to have a specific technical background to be considered.

Common Requirements

Computer: You will need an equipment that meets the company's requirements and a reliable Internet connection.

Computer Literacy: You will be expected to know how to surf the net, open windows simultaneously, use keyboard function keys, *etc.*

Keyboarding Skills: 25 wpm (words per minute) and up. Most people today meet this requirement.

Excellent Interpersonal Skills: A telephone interview will often ask "what if" types of questions. You will need to demonstrate that you can remain calm under pressure.

Landline and Headset: Your landline will have to meet specific requirements, and often you will be expected to purchase a headset.

Background Check: You will often have to pass a background check, and usually you will have to pay for this yourself.

Fingerprinting: You may be required to get fingerprinted.

How Much Can It Pay?

In the U.S. and Canada, the pay rate is generally between $9 and $14 per hour. Some companies pay by the actual time spent on the job, instead of an hourly wage. So, for example, if you spent 10 minutes talking to a customer, you would be paid for 10 minutes of work. But the time between customers would not be paid.

How to Find a Job in This Field?

You can start your job search with the websites listed in the introduction of this chapter. You can then complete your search with the following websites.

1-800 Flowers

www.1800flowers.com/about-us-employment-opportunities

2U

www.2u.com/careers/

Acanac

www.acanac.com/about-us/who-we-are/

Accolade Support

www.accoladesupport.com

ACD Direct

www.acddirect.com

Advani's

www.advanis.net/careers

Amazon

www.amazon.jobs/?location=US*

American Airlines

www.jobs.aa.com/go/Customer-Service/2537000/

American Express Company

www.careers.americanexpress.com

AnswerFirst

www.answerfirst.com

Apple

www.apple.com/jobs/us/aha.html

Apptical

www.appticaljobs.applybyweb.com/CSR/jobrequisitioninfo.html?jrid=593654

Arise Virtual Solutions

www.ariseworkfromhome.com/?utm_campaign=WAHW_LK_2017-6-16_Jposting

Aro

www.callcenteroptions.com

Arvixe

www.arvixe.com/careers

Aspire Lifestyles

www.aspirelifestyles.com

Athletic Greens

www.athleticgreens.com/pages/athletic-greens-customer-service

BloomsToday

www.bloomstoday.com/apply/contractor.php

Blue Zebra Appointment Setting

www.bluezebraappointmentsetting.com

BSG

www.bsgclearing.com/contact_us/careers/live-operator-independent-contractor

Capital One

www.capitalonecareers.com

Colony Brands

www.colonybrands.com

Concentrix

www.careers.concentrix.com/work-at-home/

ConnectAndSell

www.connectandsell.com/company/careers/

ContractWorld

www.contractxchange.com

Cruise.com

www.cruise.com

Direct Interactions

www.directinteractions.com/careers/

Enterprise

www.enterprise.com

EventBrite

www.eventbrite.com/careers/#current_positions

Groupon

www.jobs.groupon.com

Hayneedle

www.hayneedleinc.com/careers/job-openings/

HEA-Employment.com

www.hea-employment.com/job/

Hilton

www.jobs.hilton.com/select-country.php

HirePoint

hirepoint.com/athome/index.html

Hotel Tonight

www.hoteltonight.com/about/careers/

HSN

www.jobs.hsn.com

Hubstaff Talent

www.hubstaff.com/jobs

InfoCision

www.infocision.com/careers/

Intuitive Solutions

www.pizzahutishomejobs.com

JetBlue

www.jetblue.com

Kelly Services

www.kellyservices.us/us/careers/

Leadpages

www.leadpages.net/careers

Liveops

www.liveops.com

Marriott International

www.careers.marriott.com

Mondēlez International

www.mondelezinternational.com/careers

Nordstrom

www.about.nordstrom.com/careers/

Paragon Planners

www.paragonplanners.com/opportunities.php

Pleio, Inc.

www.pleio.com/careers.html

Pods

www.pods. com

RiseSmart (a Randstad Company)

www.risesmart.com/about-us/careers

Sedgwick

www.sedgwick.com/careers

Sitel

www.sitel.com/index.php?p=Careers&pageId=7

Sykes

www.sykes.com/careers-opportunities/

Service 800 inc

www.service800inc.com/careers

Synergy Solutions Inc.

www.synergysolutionsinc.com/available-positions/

Teleflora

www.myteleflora.com/careers.aspx

Teleperformance

www.teleperformance.com/en-us/jobs/estados-unidos

TeleTech

www.ttecjobs.com/en/work-from-home

UCare

www. corporatc.dow.com/en-us/careers/work-at-dow

UHaul

www.uhaul.wd1.myworkdayjobs.com/UhaulJobs

VenU

www.ven-u.com/careers/

Ver-A-Fast

www.verafast.net/job_opportunities.htm

Windy City Call Center

www.windycitycallcenter.com/careers.html

Working Solutions LLC

www.workingsolutions.com

World Travel Holdings

www.worldtravelholdings.com/careers,work-home#.WvCBJbpFx9B

Wyndham Worldwide

www.careers.wyndhamworldwide.com

XAct Telesolutions

www.myxact.com/jobs/

Xerox

www.xerox.com

As a side note, you can also work as a chat agent. I am mentioning it here as this is very similar to what a call center employee does, except you do not have to speak. You can usually find a number of these positions on the websites mentioned in the introduction of this chapter. You can also get in touch with the following company specializing in that industry:

LiveSalesStaff

www.livesalesstaff.com

7. Telemarketer

We spoke about call centers. Here we are going to discuss telemarketing positions. Although the two terms might seem synonymous for many, there are noticeable distinctions. The most important one is that telemarketers generate leads by making cold calls to promote the products or services of the client.

Common Requirements

Background: Often, companies will prefer candidates with a sales or telemarketing background. You can however find a good number of openings for beginners.

Computer: You will need an equipment that meets the company's requirements and a reliable Internet connection.

Computer Literacy: You will be expected to know how to surf the net, open windows simultaneously, use keyboard function keys, *etc.*

Excellent Interpersonal Skills: A telephone interview will often ask "what if" types of questions. You will need to demonstrate that you can remain calm under pressure.

Landline and Headset: Your landline will have to meet specific requirements, and often you will be expected to purchase a headset.

Background Check: You will often have to pass a background check, and usually you will have to pay for this yourself.

Fingerprinting: You may be required to get fingerprinted.

How much can I make?

In the U.S. and Canada, you can usually make between $9 and $14 per hour. Some companies pay by the actual time spent on the job, instead of an hourly wage. So, for example, if you spent 10 minutes talking to a customer, you will earn for 10 minutes of time. But the time between customers will not be paid.

How to Find a Job in This Field?

You can start your job search with the following websites. You can then complete your search with the websites listed in the introduction of this chapter.

A Better Call

www.abettercall.com/telemarketing_employme

nt_opportunities.html

AdviseTech Inc.

www.advisetech.com/career-opportunities/

American Support

www.jobs.americansupport.com/work-from-

home-is-the-new-cool

Arkadin (AccuConference)

www.accuconference.com/careers.html

Blue Zebra Appointment Setting

www.bluezebraappointmentsetting.com

Brighten Communications

www.brightenemployment.com/CallerInfo.aspx

Channel Blend

www.channelblend.com/were-hiring/

Cruise.com

www.cruise.com/cruise-
information/employment/

eTutorWorld

www.etutorworld.com/sales_partner_opportuni
ties.html

ExpertPlanet

www.expertplanet.com/become-an-agent

Grindstone

www.grindstone.com/join-b2b-telemarketing-
company/

Happiness Group Inc.

www.happinessgroupinc.com/join-us/current-positions/customer-happiness-team/

I Dial U

www.idialu.com/at-home-agents/

Intelliverse

www.intelliverse.com/company/careers.shtml

Lunar Cow

www.lunarcow.com/hiring_sales

Marketlink

www.marketlinc.com

Marriott International

www.careers.marriott.com

NationSwell

(Look for Community Growth Manager)

www.nationswell.com/careers/

NexRep

www.nexrep.com/agent-opportunities

Next Level Solutions

www.dial-nls.com/content.php

Oasis Marketing Solutions

www.oasismarketingsolutions.com

OPK Telemarketing Services

www.opktelemarketing.com

PhoneForce

www.phoneforce.com/careers.htm

Sage

www.careers-sage.icims.com/jobs/intro

SalesChasers

www.saleschasers.com/about-us/

SalesFish

www.salesfish.com/job_opportunities.cfm

SalesRoads

www.salesroads.com/apply.php

TeleReach

www.telereach.com

Televated, Inc.

www.televated.com/index.html

ThinkDirect

www.tdmg.com/careers/open-positions/

Welcome Wagon

www.welcomewagon.com/careers/

8. Mystery Shopper

As a mystery shopper, your job will be to pose as a customer and to evaluate goods and services. You may be asked to check the temperature of a cup of coffee, value the cleanliness of a store's restrooms, and more. The assignments may be done via the telephone, a survey, or by a visit to a location.

Mystery shopping is a legitimate work at home opportunity, and there are hundreds of mystery shopping companies, but unfortunately, a lot of scammers are involved in this industry.

Do not pay a fee to become a mystery shopper and be very wary of companies offering huge rewards. Never cash checks or money orders and send the money to the company.

Most legitimate mystery companies, though not all, are registered with the Mystery Shopping Professionals Association (MSPA). Be sure to check a company with them, but keep in mind that scammers might claim to be members, even though they are not.

Visit MSPA here: www.mspa-global.org/

Common Requirements

Computer: You will need a computer to access your emails and the Internet. You may have to fill in a spreadsheet or other online forms.

Suitable Memory: You will have to remember details of your mystery shop as you may not be able to write them down right away.

Excellent Communication: You must be able to efficiently interact with people.

Sound Writing Skills: You will need to be able to communicate the results of the mystery shop efficiently.

Reliability: Many mystery shop jobs are time sensitive. You must be able to complete the needed assignments on time.

How Much Can It Pay?

Mystery shops are paid by the job, not by the hour. The rate of pay will vary depending on the complexity of the shop. On an hourly basis, mystery shop pay works out to around $10 an hour and up. In some shops, you may receive goods and services in addition to your pay. In other cases, no fee is paid, but the shopper will receive a free meal or other assets.

How to Find a Job in This Field?

When it comes to mystery shopping, favor jobs for companies for which you can verify the reputation or the membership to a well-established professional organization.

About Face

www.aboutfacecorp.com

69

Ace Mystery Shopping

www.acemysteryshopping.com

Ann Michaels

www.ishopforyou.com

Anonymous Insights

www.a-insights.com

Automotive Insights

www.automotiveinsights.com

ARC Consulting, LLC

www.arllc.com/employment/

BestMark

www.bestmark.com/become_a_shopper.htm

Call Center QA

www.callcenterqa.org/employment/?oid=1207_1

CSR

www.csr-net.com/join-our-team/

Customer 1st

www.customer-1st.com

Customer Perspectives

www.customerperspectives.com

DSG Associates

www.dsgai.com

EXL

www.careers-exlservice.icims.com/jobs/intro?hashed=-435804125

HS Brands

www.hsbrands.com

Informa

www.financialintelligence.informa.com/contact/irs-mystery-shopper

InteliCheck, LLC

www.intelichek.com/jobs.html

IntelliShop

www.intelli-shop.com/evaluator-
area/becomean-evaluator

Jancyn

www.jancyn.com

KSS International

www.kernscheduling.com/shoppers/

Measure Consumer Perspectives

www.measurecp.com

Market Force

www.marketforce.com

North Fork Research

www.northforkresearch.com

Perception Strategies

www.perstrat.com/shopper-app/

Quality Assessments Mystery Shoppers

www.qams.com/shoppers/

Secret Shopper

www.secretshopper.com/ShopperSignup/Shopp
erSignupStart

Shoppers' Critique

www.shopperscritique.com

The Brandt Group

www.thebrandtgroup.com

Verify International

www.verifyinternational.com

9. Direct Salesperson

If you have an entrepreneurial spirit, a lot of energy, and love talking to new people, this job is probably a good fit for you. You can organize family get-togethers, for instance, to sell the wares of a company whether they're gardening supplies, bath products, wine or books, make cold calls, send emails to leads and so on. In the vast majority of the cases, you will have to create your own base of customers.

Common Requirements

There is not really any common requirement here, except your ability to sell. In most cases you will be an independent contractor. For some positions you will be required to have a specific background, which can be a medical background for instance.

How Much Can It Pay?

The amount you will receive as payment for this type of job depends on the company; however, the typical payout is about 20% to 35% of the sales. Some work from home salespersons make a six-figure salary, and some even more.

How to Find a Job in This Field?

You will have to apply to the companies directly. These companies may include the following:

Avon

www.avon.com

Carico

www.carico.com

Compelling Creations

www.compelling-creations.com

Damsel in Defense

www.damselindefense.net

Essential Bodywear

www.essentialbodywear.com

InsideSales.com

www.insidesales.com/careers/

NationSwell

www.nationswell.com/careers/

Pampered Chef

www.pamperedchef.com

Quest Software Inc.

www.quest.com/company/careers.aspx

Signature HomeStyles

www.signaturehomestyles.com

SimplyFun

www.simplyfun.com

Tealightful

www.tealightfultea.com

The Kirby Company

www.kirby.com

Thirty-One

www.mythirtyone.com

Traveling Vineyard

www.travelingvineyard.com

USBORNE Books & More

www.usbornebooksandmore.com

Younique

www.youniqueproducts.com

You can also go to the website of the Direct Selling Association (*www.dsa.org; also check www.directselling.org*) where all the companies listed accept to adhere to a set code of ethics so that they are only offering legitimate opportunities. Typically, reps make a little investment to begin, which is consistent and standard, and may sometimes have to pay a fee for the goods sold. You will find also on this platform companies operating outside the United States, listed by country.

10. Political & Advocacy Campaign Worker or Fundraiser for a Non-Profit Organization

Political organizations and candidates often need some help to convey their message or to launch a campaign. There is a lot of possible remote work in that area. Similarly, non-profit organizations are always looking to raise money to finance their activities.

Common Requirements

Computer Literacy: You will be expected to know how to use internet and sometimes conduct some research.

Excellent Interpersonal Skills: As a remote employee you will perform your work mostly over the phone, so you should be confident making cold calls, a lot of them, and you are expected to know how to engage a conversation and raise interest. You will be the "image" of the organization for the people that you will contact so the way you present yourself is very important.

Equipment: You will need a computer that meets the organization's requirements and a reliable Internet connection. Your landline will usually have to meet specific requirements, and often you will be expected to purchase a headset.

How much can I make?

You can usually expect to make between $9 and $15 per hour.

How to Find a Job in This Field?

You can start your job search with the following websites. You can then complete your search with the websites listed in the introduction of this chapter.

You will find below a few organizations hiring remote workers for political and advocacy related work.

MoveOn Political Action

www.front.moveon.org

NextWave Advocacy LLC

www.nextwaveathome.com/organize/

OnPoint@Home

www.onpointathome.com/opportunities/

People Calling People

www.peoplecallingpeople.com

If you want to explore remote fundraising opportunities you will find a number of them on websites like LinkedIn or Indeed. You can also try the following:

CAUSEWORX

www.causeworx.ca/employment/

11. Translator & Interpret

If you are also fluent in another language than English, you might be able to find a job as a translator or as an interpreter. Often people are confused between the two terms. Translators receive a document that a client needs translated in another language. These jobs may involve document translation, presentations, tutoring and more. Interprets do not write, they perform oral translations of conversations. Their work can be recorded or live. They may sometimes also work from home by video or phone conference.

You can find a lot of remote translation work if you know where to look for. There is less work for interpreter, but you can still find some.

Common Requirements

Computer: Good computer skills.

Knowledge: Fluency in another language, it comes without saying. Native fluency in another language than English is always a plus, but not an absolute requirement. Some companies require a college education, a degree in translations or an accreditation obtained through a professional organization, such as the American Translators Association but most of the time all of this isn't necessary. For the ATA, See: www.atanet.org.

Training: Experience may be required by some companies.

Communication Skill: Excellent communication skills.

How Much Can It Pay?

Pay rates vary depending on the position. Payment may be based on the number of words (be clear from the beginning if you count the number of words in the source language or in the target language!), on the number of pages or per hour. Payment can also be a flat amount negotiated between you and your client. You can work as an employee, a consultant or have your own clients. One important element to take into account is the time that you will need to complete a translation. This is relevant even if you are paid per hour. I often have clients asking me what my hourly rate is, and only after that how many hours I would need to finish the job. If I say too little, I can end up working for very little per hour, and if I estimate too many hours I can lose the client. Assessing your time is common sense but you can easily run into translation issues with a work or an expression that does not exist in the target language and it may not look like it, but this can easily increase the number of hours needed. Marketing documents or sales related document can be very challenging sometimes. So, a word of advice: always ask to see the document or a sample of it and take a close eye to the terminology.

A note on certified translations: from time to time you will run into a job description mentioning certified translations. If you do not know what this is, you might just pass up on a great project. In the United States, anybody who can sign a statement indicating that he or she is fluent in English and in the other appropriate language can certify that the document is accurate to the best of his knowledge and ability. And that's all there is. Often this statement will have to be notarized in front of a public notary, which can usually be done for free at any branch at your bank. They always have a public notary on site and if you are a client, often they do not ask for you to pay for it. At least, I have done it many times myself and I have never paid anything.

How to Find a Job in This Field?

You can start your job search with the websites listed in the introduction of this chapter. You can then complete your search with the following websites.

Gengo, Inc.

www.gengo.com/translators/

Academic Word

www.academicword.com/emp.asp

LanguageLine Solutions

www.languageline.com/company/careers/interp reter-careers/

Language Translation

www.languagetranslation.com

Linguistic Systems Inc.

www.linguist.com

NetworkOmni

www.networkomni.com/about-careers.asp

Pacific Interpreters

www.pacificinterpreters.com/careers

Responsive Translation Services

www.responsivetranslation.com

Telelanguage

www.telelanguage.com/careers

Translators Town Limited

www.translatorstown.com

UC Translations

www.uctranslations.com

VerbalizeIt Inc.

www.verbalizeit.com/become-a-translator/

Finally, I also email translation companies that I can find on internet, even if there is no opening listed or if the company seems very small. I also attend networking events organized by chambers of commerce, in particular foreign chambers of commerce such as the French American Chamber of Commerce (since my other language is French, *Et Oui!*), but it can be anything else (the Italian American Chamber of Commerce, the Spain-U.S. Chamber of Commerce, just name it).

12. English Trainer or Teacher

Many people are making money online by teaching English. English is a language that is in demand around the world, so having it as your first language is a skill you can use to earn. Some choose to move to China or Korea for a year or two to teach English, but you don't have to drive across the world to take advantage of these opportunities. There are many students in countries like Korea, Japan, Germany and France, just to name a few, who are looking for English speakers to help them learn spoken English by way of conversation.

The sessions may focus on things like running a meeting, making professional small talk or negotiating a contract. As a trainer, you'll get details on how to teach every topic, and you will receive a short training before starting the job. You will find the office experience very helpful, if you have some, because many students work in a corporate environment.

Students are also supplementing their traditional education with online products and apps centered on education, and countless adults are opting for taking classes online instead of in person to develop general conversation skills.

If you're a native English speaker, have necessary computer skills, an interest in other cultures, and love chatting over the phone or online, this might be the perfect job for you.

The lessons themselves will usually happen on a live internet video service such as Skype, or over the phone.

Common Requirements:

Education & Professional Skills: In most of the cases you must be a native speaker. If you're from the United States, Canada, the United Kingdom, or another English-speaking nation, you already have a distinct advantage! Necessarily, the majority of you who have found your way to this book would be eligible to teach

English on the internet. Some, but not all, platforms desire English teachers that already have experience teaching, but requiring experience is not very common when it comes to online education. As long as you are willing to learn how to teach you will find many job openings for you. In addition, some companies may require a degree or a certificate in teaching, but this is the exception rather than the rule. Again, this is a fairly open position.

Being bilingual is automatically a plus but is usually not required. Most of the platforms online don't require the English teachers they employ to know the language of the students they're teaching, although it's considered a strength and asset for the job.

Age: Most online English teaching jobs require that you are at least 16 years old, but some might want you to be 18.

Equipment: This job requires you to have a computer, a phone and a headset to use Skype. This job requires that you have a steady internet connection that will support video functions for online chat lessons. Many of these jobs will want you to have PayPal or something similar that allows you to accept online payments for your work.

Schedule: If it's open and flexible you have an advantage. Since the students you'll be working with are in different time zones, you should expect to work at night sometimes.

How Much Can It Pay?

This job can pay about $12 to $22 per hour and you often as many or as little hours as you want.

How to Find a Job in This Field?

To start your job search, you can begin with goFLUENT (www.*gofluent.com)*, an English training company that works with twelve of the most prominent corporations in the world. You can also find a job as an ESL (English as a second language) teacher — these are more structured. For that you can visit the webstite of Learnlight: www.learnlight.com.

You can also visit the following websites:

Berlitz

www.berlitz.us

Blue Media LLC *(BuddySchool)*

www.buddyschool.com/faq#20

Cambly Inc.

www.cambly.com

Continuum Education Services

www.continuumservices.org

Englishunt Inc

www.englishuntusa.com

Ginseng English, Inc

www.ginsengenglish.com

Golden Voice English

www.gveoe.com

Italki HK Limited

www.italki.com/teacher/application

iTutor.com Inc.

www.itutor.com

Lingoda GmgH

www.lingoda.com

Pearson

www.pearson.com

TeachPartTime.com

www.teachparttime.com

Rosetta Stone

www.rosettastone.com

Rype, Inc.

www.rypeapp.com

TalktoCanada

www.talktocanada.com/careers/

VIPKID Beijing ICP

www.vipkidteachers.com

Topic-Time

www.topic-time.com/en

TutorABC

www. tutorabc.com

Tutor In Ltd

www.twosigmas.com

Verbalplanet.com

www.verbalplanet.com/tutorhome.asp

Verbling

www.verbling.com/teach

Voxy

www.voxy.com

13. Tutor

Students need tutors for a variety of subjects. These include elementary through college tutoring, test prep, and more.

Common Requirements

Education: A number of tutoring companies require a teaching certificate. They may accept one that is expired, but not if it was revoked for any reason. Some will accept college students as well. In some cases, you will have to pass an exam that demonstrates your ability in the subject matter.

Computer: You will need a laptop that meets their requirements with a reliable Internet connection.

Computer Literacy: You should be comfortable using a computer.

Good Teaching Skills: Interviews that will be conducted usually include role-playing situations, to see how you may react. You may be expected to pass tests demonstrating your knowledge over the phone as well.

Headset: You will often be expected to purchase a headset.

Background Check: You will have to pass a background check. This is usually paid for by the hiring company, but not always.

Fingerprinting: You will often be required to get fingerprinted.

How Much Can It Pay?

Many companies pay an hourly wage to tutors. This may be determined by the subject matter taught. Other companies allow the tutor to set their rate and collect a percentage.

How to Find a Job in This Field?

Here, I would start my job search with the websites in this section. You can of course browse the list of websites provided in the introduction of this chapter but if you want to be time-efficient it's better to start here first.

Aim-for-A-Tutoring

www.aim4a.com/tutors.php

Blue Media LLC *(BuddySchool)*

www.buddyschool.com/faq#20

Brainfuse Inc.

www.brainfuse.com/register/becomtutor.asp

Connections Academy

www.connectionsacademy.com/careers/home.aspx

eTutorWorld Corporation

www.etutorworld.net

Growing Stars

www.growingstars.com

Measurement Incorporated

www.measurementinc.com/careers

Meteor Learning

www.meteorlearning.com/#/jobs

Pearson

www.pearson.com/us/

Tutor

www.tutor.com/apply/application-process

Tutorvista

www.tutorvista.com/teaching-jobs

14. Online or Remote Expert

I am sure that you have already been in a situation where you needed an information or an advice quickly and did not know where to find it. This is where your online or remote expert jumps in. Several companies have developed websites and apps allowing registered users to ask questions on all kind of subjects to a variety of users. In order to become an expert you may need a specific background that you might or might not have, such as being a licensed attorney, a doctor or an engineer. If you are qualified you can sign up now to become an expert. However, you will find a number of questions that are more accessible, like questions from students, general technical questions for which you can find the answer on internet, or lifestyle related questions.

Common Requirements

Education & Background: There is no common requirement as to the level of education and background here as it depends on the type of questions to answer and on the platform. That being said, you can be an expert in virtually anything. If you have cooking skills for instance there might be somebody waiting for an answer from you. So, check these websites!

English Language Skills: You must have excellent English language skills, grammar, and spelling.

Equipment: Rather minimal. You need to have a computer with an internet connection. A cell phone with an internet connection is a plus as it allows you to answer questions at any time and from anywhere. In addition, if you use some platforms you will have to answer by phone, not in writing.

How Much Can It Pay?

It all depends on the platform, subject matter of the questions, and on the time you devote to that activity. It can go from a few cents per question to a six-figure salary per year. The range is fairly broad.

How to Find a Job in This Field?

If you want to become an online expert, you can take a look at the following websites:

1Q

www.1q.com

6ya

www.6ya.com/experts

Clarity

www.clarity.fm/help/articles/2/how-does-clarity-work

Fixya

www.fixya.com

JustAnwer

www.justanswer.com

OnFrontiers

www.onfrontiers.com/become-an-expert

PrestoExperts

www.prestoexperts.com

Promeets Technology Corp.

www. commongenius.com/expert-consultant/signup

StudyPool

www.studypool.com/online-tutor-job

Tutor

www.tutor.com/apply

Wonder

www.askwonder.com/researcher

Yup

www.yup.com/become-tutor

15. Writer

Writers are needed for a wide range of assignments. From writing product reviews to short stories, to blog posts and more, there is always a need for quality writers.

Common Requirements

Compute: You will need to communicate with your client, write your material, and be able to do necessary research online.

English Language Skills: You will need to have *excellent* English language skills, grammar, and spelling.

Writing Ability: You should be able to write quality material in a way that engages the reader.

Knowledge: You will need to know the subject matter you are writing about, or have the ability to research it.

How Much Can It Pay?

Writers get paid differently depending on the company or individual client. Writers may be paid per word, a flat rate per article, a percentage of clicks and views on the report, or a set salary.

If you decide to do freelance work, make sure that you get paid at least half up front, unless you use a platform that puts your payment into escrow until full completion of your work and which has dispute resolution rules in place, just in case (e.g. www.upwork.com).

How to Find a Job in This Field?

The following is a list of companies that hire writers directly or share writer job listings that have an upfront payment (meaning that the payment is not based on the number of views or clicks):

$99 Social *(full-time position)*

www.99dollarsocial.com/content-specialist-
position/

Anxiety Foundation

www.anxietyfoundation.com/contributors/

b. michelle pippin

www.bmichellepippin.com/get-paid-to-share-
your-expertise-with-us/

bitchmedia

www.bitchmedia.org/writers-guidelines

BKA Content

www.bkacontent.com/write-for-bka/

Blogmutt

www.blogmutt.com/become-a-writer

BookBrowse

www.bookbrowse.com/reviewers/index.cfm/fus
eaction/apply

Book in a Box

www.bookinabox.com/freelancer/

Content Divas

www.contentdivas.com/write-for-content-divas/

Cosmopolitan

www.surveymonkey.com/r/?sm=P%2bTI3UALB
1rlCBgvlYElag%3d%3d

Crowd Content

www.crowdcontent.com/author/sign-up/step/1

Cultures + Cuisines

www.culturesandcuisines.com/submissions/

Doctor Of Credit

www.doctorofcredit.com/want-to-write-and-get-paid-for-doctor-of-credit/

Domainite

www.domainite.com/writing-sample/

eCommerce Insiders

www.ecommerceinsiders.com/write/

Eureka Street

www.eurekastreet.com.au/article.aspx?aeid=339
27#.VjraH2SrToz

Expatica

www.expatica.com/editorial-policy.html

FreelanceMom

www.freelancemom.com/guest-post-guidelines/

Freelance Writing

www.freelancewriting.com

Freelance Writing Gigs

www.freelancewritinggigs.com

getabstract

www.getabstract.com/en/writers/application

Guideposts

www.guideposts.org/writers-guidelines

iHire, LLC

www.ihirepublishing.com

IncomeDiary

www.incomediary.com/write-for-incomediary

iWriter

www.iwriter.com

Jobtomic.com

www.jobtomic.com/jobs/index.jsp

Journalism Jobs

www.journalismjobs.com/job-listings

JustParents

www.justparents.co.uk/write-for-justparents/

Knitty

www.knitty.com/subguide.php

Konsus

www.konsus.com/career

ListVerse

www.listverse.com/write-get-paid/

Metro Parent

www.metroparent.com/write-us/

Narratively

www.narratively.submittable.com/submit

NextWave Advocacy LLC

www.nextwaveathome.com/write/

OpenSpace

www.crowdsource.com/workforce/

Problogger.com

www.problogger.com/jobs/

Saveur

www.saveur.com/contact

skirt! Magazine

www.skirt.com/contribute/

Sun Oasis

www.sunoasis.com/freelance.html

Tablet

www.tabletmag.com/about

Textbroker

www.textbroker.com/authors

The Content Authority

www.thecontentauthority.com

The Establishment

www.theestablishment.co/pitch-us-
b0788d803a0b

The Penny Hoarder

www.thepennyhoarder.com/contributor-
guidelines/

Wordgigs.com

www.wordgigs.com

Wow!

www.wow-womenonwriting.com/contact.php

Your Tango

www.yourtango.com/submissions

16. Proofreader & Editor

Virtually any company publishing written content, whether online or not, needs people to review the work before publication. This is what proofreaders and editors do. If you are a good writer and are meticulous when it comes to commas, periods and spelling, then you might want to take a closer look at your options here. You do not necessarily need experience in this field to find a job.

Common Requirements

English Language Skills: You will need to have excellent English language skills, grammar, and spelling. You must also be very details-oriented.

Equipment: You need a computer and an internet connection. You might want to have a printer also as it sometimes makes sense to print a hard copy of your work.

How Much Can It Pay?

Proofreaders and editors get paid differently depending on the company or individual client. They may be paid per word, a flat rate or a set salary.

Like for writers, if you opt to do freelance work, make sure that you get paid at least half up front, unless you use a platform that puts your payment into escrow until full completion of your work and that has rules in place in case of a dispute with the client (for instance: www.upwork.com).

If you are a highly skilled proofreader or editor, usually with at least a PhD, you can expect to earn more. I have listed a few websites for highly qualified individuals.

How to Find a Job in This Field?

The following is a list of companies that hire proofreaders and editors. Feel free to complete your search also with the list of websites mentioned in the introduction of this chapter.

Book in a Box

www.bookinabox.com/freelancer/

Cactus Communications

www.cactusglobal.com/careers/work-from-home#wfh

Crowd Content

www.crowdcontent.com/author/sign-up/step/1

Domainite

www.domainite.com/editing-sample/

Edit911 *(for highly qualified editors)*

www.edit911.com/employment/

EditFast

www.editfast.com/english/editjobs.htm

Editor World LLC

www.editorworld.com/register/editor

Enago

www.enago.com/careers/current-openings.htm

English Trackers *(for highly qualified editors)*

www.englishtrackers.com/about-us/join-us

Gramlee

www.gramlee.com/jobs.html

IXL Learning

www.ixl.com/company/jobs

Jobtomic.com

www.jobtomic.com/jobs/index.jsp

Kibin

www.kibin.com/proofreading-jobs

Kirkus

www.kirkusreviews.com/about/careers/

Laika Ventures LLC

www.proofreadingservices.com/pages/careers

LifeTips

www.lifetips.com/about/join-team-editorial.html

Polished Paper *(for highly qualified editors)*

www.polishedpaper.com/editor/register

ProofreadingPal LLC

www.proofreadingpal.com/proofreading-career-opportunities.php

Proofread*NOW*.com

www.proofreadnow.com/employment

Research Square

www.rscontractors.theresumator.com

Scribendi

www.scribendi.com/employment.en.html

Sibia Proofreading

www.sibiaproofreading.com/become-an-editor.html

Wordfirm Inc.

www.managedediting.com/freelance-work.html

Wordy *(will resume hiring during Q2 or Q3 2018)*

www.wordy.com/wordy-for-editors

WORDSRU *(for highly qualified editors)*

www.wordsru.com/jobs

17. Copywriter

Copywriters are a specific category of writers and this job requires specific skills. Copywriters focus on writing advertisements and other forms of marketing materials to promote a product, a service or a company. This is essentially a marketing job. Copywriters are also sometimes called "salesmen in print." Their work has nothing to do with copyrights, even if their work can be copyrighted. They are called copywriters because their job consists in writing a copy, the word used in that industry to designate a promotional text.

Common Requirements

Education: In general, you will need a bachelor's degree in a field establishing your ability to write (e.g. English or journalism) and/or to market a product, service or company (e.g. advertising or marketing).

Professional Skills: You need to have excellent English language skills, grammar, and spelling, but that's not all. You also need to be a detail-oriented person. You must be your own proofreader. Copywriters need to have excellent research skills as well and to understand the needs of the clients.

Equipment: You simply need a computer and a cell phone. If your clients are located abroad, you might want to invest in a headset and some Skype credits if you need to call but most of the time this will not be necessary.

How Much Can It Pay?

A freelance copywriter can in general make anywhere from $25 per hour to $60. If your work product is really outstanding, you can ask for more. Some copywriters ask for $130 per hour. It really depends on the quality of your work. If you work as an employee the pay will be less, count around $25 to $35 per hour in general.

How to Find a Job in This Field?

You can start your job search with the websites listed in the introduction of this chapter. You can then complete your search with the following websites.

American Writers & Artists Inc.

www.directresponsejobs.com

Cloud Peeps Inc.

www.cloudpeeps.com

Copyfy

https://uk.copify.com/

Coyne & Blanchard, Inc. (creativehotlist)

www.creativehotlist.com

Jobtomic.com

www.jobtomic.com/jobs/index.jsp

Mediabistro, Inc.

www.mediabistro.com

PowerToFly

www.powertofly.com/jobs/page/1/?submit=Filter
&location_type=Remote&location_type=Hybrid

Problogger.com

www.problogger.com/jobs/

18. Grant Writer

What is a grant writer? As it sounds, a grand writer is person specializing in grant applications for the benefit of her employer or clients. Many public institutions or private organizations offer these grants for a variety of causes or purposes and the grant writer's job is to use his writing skills to assist other entities or individuals in securing these funds. Charities and nonprofit organizations use the services of grant writers all the time to help finance their activities.

Common Requirements

Education & Background: You will usually need at least a bachelor's degree to work in that field. You can start working remotely as an entry-level grant writer but employers and clients will often prefer a writer who has a few years of experience. Writing grant proposals is more complex than one might think. It requires a good understanding of the process, of the audience and the ability to research the necessary information to prepare a successful submission. It's more than simply writing a request to obtain a funding.

English Language Skills: You must have excellent English language skills, grammar, and spelling.

Knowledge & Professional Skills: You need to be comfortable working with the Microsoft office suit but if you have bachelor's degree you are probably an expert already. Grant writers must be very organized in their work, have creative writing skills and be able to follow each and every guideline specified by the grantor. They also need to adapt their proposals and to use the language that's the most adapted to the grant they apply for.

Equipment: This is very basic. Mostly a computer, preferably a laptop, an internet connection and a cell phone.

How Much Can It Pay?

According to glassdoor.com, the average salary for grant writers in the United States is a little under $50,000 per year.

(www.glassdoor.com/Salaries/us-grant-writer-salary-SRCH_IL.0,2_IN1_KO3,15.htm)

How to Find a Job in This Field?

You can start your job search with the websites listed in the introduction of this chapter. You can then complete your search with the following websites.

Associated Grant Makers

www.agmconnect.org/jobs

Association of Fundraising Professionals

www.afpnet.org *(check job section)*

Elysian Trust

www.elysiantrust.org/wp/grantworkerteam

Grant Professionals Association

www.grantprofessionals.org *(check job section)*

Jobs2Careers

www.jobs2careers.com/Jobs/q-Remote-Grant-Writer/

Side Income Jobs

www.sideincomejobs.com

Society for Nonprofits

www.snpo.org/nonprofitcareers/jobresults2.php

19. Social Media Manager

If you are an experienced social media user (most people are today!) you may want to investigate social media manager opportunities. Many of these jobs are remote jobs. If you already manage your own social media or have experience doing it for others this is of course an asset in your job search. If not, you have countless websites on internet where you can find valuable (free) information to get you started.

What does a social media manager do in practice?

A social media manager is a person who manages the online presence of a company and/or a product, monitoring online activity and content, generating traffic, attracting influencers, SEO... This is basically a marketing position, with sometimes a customer service aspect when asked to handle customer complaints as well. A social media manager may be asked to monitor media accounts that have already been set up by a company, or to create one from scratch.

Common Requirements:

Compute: You will need to communicate with your client, write the materials, and be able to do necessary research online.

116

English Language Skills: You will need to have excellent English language skills, grammar, and spelling.

Time Management Skills: You must be organized and know how to prioritize tasks to be successful.

Knowledge: You will need a deep understanding of the most common social media platforms: Facebook, Twitter, Instagram, Pinterest, LinkedIn, but also Youtube, Dailymotion and more. A background in marketing, while useful, is not necessarily required. Many social media managers have never attended a marketing class (which does not mean that you should not educate yourself).

How Much Can It Pay?

Social media managers who work as consultants set their own fees. They are based on the number of hours of work requested or expected and on the target and benefits that they bring to the client. This can range from a few hundred dollars per month per client to a several thousands. Usually social media managers can expect to be paid between $15 and $50 per hour. Social Media Managers manage their own business and can therefore have several clients at the same time, unless they sign an exclusivity contract but this unusual. You can also receive a bonus, or a share of the profits generated.

How to Find a Job in This Field?

Most of these jobs can be found using the list of websites provided in the introduction of this chapter, like LinkedIn or Craigslist. You can also look at the following websites to find more opportunities:

Cloud Peeps Inc.

www.cloudpeeps.com

CMX

www.cmxhub.com/jobs/

Freelancermap GmbH

(Some jobs for English speakers)

www.freelancermap.com

Outsourcely

www.outsourcely.com/remote-workers

If you want to start a business in this field, you may want to attend business networking events in your area and distribute your business card around you. Your clients can be large or small companies, so do not restrict yourself to businesses that are already present on the internet! Start-up companies are good candidates for the type of services that you offer. If you know of any in your area you might want to get in touch with them.

20. Community Moderator

Community moderators are often confused with social media managers, but the two roles are distinct. Community moderators are only in charge of the content posted on a social media network. They do not promote, they monitor what other members can post for things like unrelated content, spam, offensive and illegal contents. This job can also be done by social media managers but their primary focus is really on promoting the social media channel and on generating as much quality traffic as possible. A community moderator can also be asked to review and implement the policies applicable to the members.

Common Requirements

English Language Skills: You need to have a good understanding of the English language and you must be able to write correct English. It's also an advantage if you have a good understanding of cultural references.

Knowledge: You do not necessarily to have a good understanding of the most common social media platforms, such as Facebook, Twitter, Instagram and/or Pinterest, but you must at least show that you can learn quickly and can work independently. You can also work as a moderator on many other platforms and forums, some rather confidential.

How Much Can It Pay?

Community moderators are often paid between $8 and $15 per hour. You might find job listings offering more but this is less common. Your pay will also depend on whether you are an employee or an independent contractor.

How to Find a Job in This Field?

You can start your job search with the following websites. You can then complete your search with the websites listed in the introduction of this chapter.

CMX

www.cmxhub.com/jobs/#s=1

LiveWorld *(bilingual positions)*

www.liveworld.com/about-us/#careers

Modsquad

www.modsquad.com/join-the-mods/?gnk=job&gni=8a7884494ed83777014ef49c14b25318

Remoters

www.remoters.net/jobs/freelance-community-manager-blogger/

21. Health Care Positions

Health care professionals are always in demand, and the opportunities online are expanding. Positions include health insurance representative, health coach, medical transcription, medical coders and more. There are some positions for telecommuting nurses, including insurance case managers and telephone health advisors.

Common Requirements

Education: Most healthcare positions require a degree and a training. Though there are some telecommute jobs for Licensed Practical Nurses, most are for Registered Nurses. In addition, a state license is required.

Experience: Many telecommute healthcare positions require several years of hands-on experience.

Interpersonal Skills: Excellent interpersonal skills with the ability to work well under pressure are needed.

How Much Can It Pay?

These highly skilled healthcare jobs are some of the highest paying work from home jobs. Registered nurses can earn thousands per month, and work at home physicians can take in as much as there in-office counterparts. Medical coders can also make a very decent salary and they job is in very high demand.

How to Find a Job in This Field?

You can start your job search with the websites listed in the introduction of this chapter. You can then complete your search with the following websites.

American Red Cross

www.redcross.org

AmeriHealth Caritas

www.amerihealthcaritas.com

Anthem

www.antheminc.com

Centene Corporation

www.centene.com

Imaging On Call

www.radnet.com/imaging-on-call/

Mckesson

www.mckesson.com/en_us/McKesson.com/Careers/Careers.html

Parameds

www.parameds.com/join.html

Permedion

http://hmspermedion.com/careers

SironaHealth

www.sironahealth.com/careers

Tenet Healthcare Corporation

www.jobs.tenethealth.com/search-jobs/remote

Verscend Technologies, Inc.

www.ultimatesoftware.com/careers/

22. Accounting and Bookkeeping

Bookkeeping and accounting positions, such as tax preparation, payroll, client financials, and more, are available remotely. For these positions, employers will often seek and prefer qualified individuals. However, bookkeeping offers may be available to beginners with no specific background in accounting. While it may sound like a complex job at first, the basics of bookkeeping can be learned in very little time and some employers will provide the necessary training.

Common Requirements

Education: Many companies will require a college degree, and some will ask you to be a CPA (Certified Public Accountant) for the most complex tasks.

Experience: Experience is often a requirement for work at home accounting and bookkeeping positions, and the more the better, of course. That being said, as already mentioned, you can find remote entry-level bookkeeper positions.

Specialized Knowledge: Knowledge of financial software such as Quick Books is often preferred, but not always required.

Communication: Excellent communication skills are required, along with the ability to meet the needs of the client base.

How Much Can It Pay?

Pay will depend on the company, your skills level, and qualifications. One company quotes a pay rate of $2,000 per month for 15-20 hours, with more for complex assignments for accounting professionals. Another company offers some benefits, including a matched 401K plan along with a competitive salary. Most bookkeeper jobs you will see pay between $13 and $23 per hour. CPAs can earn a lot more.

How to Find a Job in This Field?

You can start your job search with the websites listed in the introduction of this chapter. You can then complete your search with the following websites.

AccountingDepartment.com

www.accountingdepartment.com/jobs/

Bateman & Co., Inc.

www.batemanhouston.com/employme.htm

Belay, Inc.

www.belaysolutions.com/our-company/work-with-us/

Click Accounts

www.clickaccounts.com/whoweare_careers.html

CPA Moms

www.members.cpa-moms.com/find-a-client/

Intuit

www.careers.intuit.com/professional

23. Paralegal and Legal Secretary

A paralegal is a person working for an attorney under his supervision and his control. You might sometimes see people advertising their services as paralegal services but working independently. There is no such thing in the United States as an independent paralegal. A paralegal MUST work for an attorney or under his supervision. A paralegal performs legal tasks, like writing a contract, conducting a legal research, preparing forms for a client, making phone calls, organizing meetings and many things that you could expect a lawyer to do. In other words, they perform substantive work. In fact, when you hire a lawyer, you will often work hand-to-hand with his paralegal(s). Paralegals are sometimes referred to as legal assistants.

You sometimes see individuals introducing themselves as paralegals, for instance in the area of immigration law. Often, they do not realize that the mere act of telling what form their clients should complete and submit to receive some immigration benefit is reserved to licensed attorneys. In other words, they expose themselves to legal troubles for unlawfully practicing law.

That being said, paralegals do not necessarily have to work on-site, from the lawyer's office.

Unlike paralegals, legal secretaries do not perform substantive work. Their work is more administrative in nature. Legal secretaries answer phone calls, manage the lawyer's calendar, type letters and legal documents, arrange meetings, help filing documents and other similar tasks.

Common Requirements:

Education: For paralegals, a paralegal certificate is a strong asset, but not required. If you are motivated and show interest for the position or if you are contemplating a career in law as a lawyer you might be able to start working as a paralegal. A bachelor's degree is usually preferred, but in practice many paralegals have an associate degree in paralegal studies. For legal secretaries, a high-school degree is usually sufficient, but a legal secretary certificate is an asset.

English Language Skills: You must have excellent English language skills, grammar, and spelling.

Knowledge & Professional Skills: For paralegal positions you need to be comfortable using a computer and the Microsoft office suit. If you are knowledgeable about Lexis Nexis and Westlaw, this is huge plus. Also, you need to be comfortable calling clients and sometimes other law firms. For legal secretary positions you need advanced computer skills. through the same channels than the ones mentioned for paralegal jobs.

How Much Can It Pay?

You can usually expect to be paid between $12 and $25 per hour depending on your profile and experience.

How to Find a Job in This Field?

Most paralegal and legal secretary jobs will be on-site, but you can nevertheless find remote paralegal positions. The law industry has been engaged in a huge outsourcing trend for several years now. Law firms try to cut their costs as much as possible to remain competitive and simply put to try to survive in a very competitive sector.

You can always contact small law firms advertising an on-site position or a part-time position. Part-time positions are often a sign that the firm is small (e.g. solo practitioner or just a few attorneys) and this might be your chance. If you offer to work for less (not for free!) but from home, or mostly from home, this might be a compelling argument for a lawyer trying to keep his expenses as low as possible.

Understand, one key point here. A crucial concept in law related jobs is the concept of conflict of interest. In just few words, this means that once you represent a client, or work for a lawyer representing a client, your ability to work for the other party becomes limited. A waiver may be possible, but do not count on it. What does that mean for you? This is simple. If you work as a paralegal part-time for a law firm and you really want to work full-time, it's going to be very difficult for you to find a job at another law firm if you disclose your employment status. Most lawyers will not accept that situation, in particular since the mere appearance of an inappropriate situation is not allowed. Let's be clear, I am _not_ saying that you should keep that information secret from another employer, quite the contrary. Simply understand that it's likely going to be very difficult to cumulate a job at two law firms if you take a part-time position. It's probably easier and safer to just find another activity that you will be able to do when not working as a paralegal. Keep in mind that even that should be disclosed to your employer.

The best websites to find remote paralegal jobs are the platforms mentioned in the introduction of this chapter. Indeed.com in particular is a good place to start your search and one to check frequently.

You can also check the website of the various state bar organizations as they often have a job board that you can check for free. In addition, you can take a look at the following websites:

Red Hat, Inc.

(Search for Contracts Administrator)

www.careers-redhat.icims.com/jobs/search

SimplyHire

www.simplyhired.com

24. Online Juror

We all know that serving as a juror does not pay very well, but serving as an online juror is a different story. And you have none of the inconvenience, like missing days of work, waiting for hours, if not days, to know whether you are selected or not, and so on.

What exactly is an online juror? An online juror is a person who is going to provide his opinion on a case based on documents provided to him, in order for a law firm to have a sense of where the opinion can go on a particular matter in a particular jurisdiction. If you want, this is like taking part to an online survey except that it's focusing on a legal matter. It helps lawyers and law firms prepare cases for litigation or settlement. The panel is usually significantly larger than for a real jury. It can be made up of a few dozens of people to help the lawyers have a broader understanding of what people think in a particular area about a specific topic. As you can imagine, depending on where you live you will have more or less chance to be selected as some area will have more cases than others or more competition to be chosen.

Common Requirements:

The requirements to become an online juror are the same than the ones you would need to meet to become a real juror. Therefore, you must be a U.S. Citizen and be over 18-year-old. There is no requirement regarding your level of education, however you must be able to understand the English language. You must also live in the required jurisdiction. Some sites make an exception for the U.S. citizens living abroad if they still have an address in the United States, in which case they will be considered as living at this address. You must not have been convicted and you cannot be a lawyer, and sometimes even a family member of a lawyer (even if in the real life, a lawyer may be selected as a juror). You will usually have to complete a demographic form, a little like what you receive from the court house when invited to attend jury selection. That information will be kept confidential, but double check the site policies as this can change with no notice.

How Much Can It Pay?

Being an online juror will likely not bring you enough money to make a living just from that activity. However, for the time spent on each case the pay rate is fairly good. The time you are usually going to spend reviewing a case is going to go from 20 minutes to an hour, and for that you can expect to be paid $20 to $60. In other words, you can be paid a dollar a minute. Not so bad. This is of course going to vary from one company to another and from one case to another. This is just to give you a sense. Also, you will not be considered an employee but an independent contractor, unless otherwise stated.

How to Find a Job in This Field?

If you would like to supplement your income by working as an online juror, you can register or enter your email address on the following websites to be notified when a case becomes available:

eJury.com

www.ejury.com

JuryTest Networks

www.jurytest.net/index.cfm?action=howjur

Online Verdict

www.onlineverdict.com/jurors/

Resolution Research & Marketing Inc.

www.resolutionresearch.com/page/recruitment

-mock-jury

VirtualJury.com

www.virtualjury.com/jurors_about_virtual_jury.

asp

25. Survey Taker

There is nothing easier than to take a survey. If you are fluent enough in English and can understand the questions, then you can take survey to make earn money.

This job may require you to fill out an opinion poll, answer questions concerning shopping habits, or even review a particular product. You can then be paid in cash (mailed directly to you or paid via PayPal), or with points that you can redeem for gift cards.

Common Requirements:

Background: You will not be eligible to take all the surveys available. Each survey has its own specific requirements. It can require that you do your shopping two times a week, own a car, took holidays in the last 12 months, be over a certain age or any other type of requirement you can possibly think about. These surveys are conducted because companies want to learn about you, as their market target. If you are not eligible, just move on to another survey, there are more available than you can possibly complete.

Equipment: You need a computer or a cell phone with a good internet connection. If you were to be disconnected in the middle of a survey you might lose the benefit of the time spend completing it.

How Much Can It Pay?

This job can pay anywhere from $1 to $50 per survey completed. Keep in mind that you must take into account the amount of time required to complete the study. Many companies offer just a few cents. This is usually not worth your time. Focus on surveys that pay decently. If you are good at multitasking, you can take surveys while doing other tasks, like answering telephone calls.

How to Find a Job in This Field?

Simply visit platforms such the ones listed below then sign up with the sites available (as many as you can). These platforms will contact you when surveys are fitting your demographic pop up; you can then take them immediately and earn the reward.

Bridge Entertainment, Inc.

www.epollsurveys.com

CashCrate.com

www.cashcrate.com

Darwin's Data

www.darwinsdata.com

IGain LLC

www.vindale.com

Ipsos

www.ipsos.com/en

Lightspeed

www.globaltestmarket.com

www.mysurvey.com

Luth Research LLC

www.surveysavvy.com

MindSwarms

www.mindswarms.com

OnePoll Ltd

www.onepoll.com

PineCone Research

www.pineconeresearch.com

Prodege, LLC

www.swagbucks.com

Survey Sampling International, LLC

www.ipoll.com

www.opinionoutpost.com

www.surveyspot.com

The NPD Group, Inc.

www.vipvoice.com

Umongous, Inc.

www.paidviewpoint.com

Valued Opinions

www.valuedopinions.com

TIP: Do not register on any platform that asks for a membership fee or that requests your bank info or social security number. Any site that is vague about payment should also not be an option.

26. Remote Surveyor, Interviewer or Data Collection Agent

We spoke about taking surveys. Here we are going to switch seats. You can work from home (or from wherever you want) calling people to make *them* answer survey questionnaires. Indeed, a number of companies hire remote employees or independent contractors in order to conduct surveys, to interview people or to collect data for market research purposes.

The requirements and pay will be similar to what you can expect to make if you work as a customer service representative.

Common Requirements

Computer: You will need an equipment that meets the company's requirements and a reliable Internet connection.

Computer Literacy: You will be expected to know how to surf the net, open windows simultaneously, use keyboard function keys, *etc.*

Excellent Interpersonal Skills: A telephone interview will often ask "what if" types of questions. You will need to demonstrate that you can remain calm under pressure.

Landline and Headset: Your landline will have to meet specific requirements, and often you will be expected to purchase a headset.

Background Check: You will often have to pass a background check, and usually you will have to pay for this yourself.

Fingerprinting: You may be required to get fingerprinted.

How much can I make?

In the U.S. and Canada, you can usually make between $9 and $14 per hour.

How to Find a Job in This Field?

You can start your job search with the following websites. You can then complete your search with the websites listed in the introduction of this chapter.

Advanis

www.advanis.net/careers

SSRS (surveys)

www.ssrs.com/careers/

Telecare Corporation

www.telcarecorp.com/about-us/career-opportunities/

Westat, Inc

www.westat.com/careers

Yardi Matrix

www.yardirentsurvey.wordpress.com

27. Babysitting

Babysitting is a classic work from home job. You can work as an employee or operate your own business from the comfort of your home or apartment. You might or might not need a license to work depending on the local regulations in place where you live and on the specifics of what you intend to do. Above a certain number of children and a certain number of hours that they spend in your dwelling expect to have to apply for a license, which will usually require that you meet certain training and/or education requirements. The place where you will keep the children will also usually need to adhere to certain standards for safety reasons.

Common Requirements:

Education: There is no minimum requirement in terms of level of education to become a babysitter or a nanny. However, to stand out of

140

the competition, it's always an advantage to have a childcare qualification and a CPR certification. If you speak a foreign language, make it clear as it can be an appealing argument for parents. If your activity requires a license, then you will have to meet the minimum education and training requirements.

Equipment: It's advisable to have a computer and an internet connection, or at the very least to have the possibility to access to your emails as you increase your chances to find a family if you advertise your services on specialized websites. The bare minimum is a cell phone with the possibility to send emails from it. Many parents want to know what is going on with their kids while you are taking care of them. If you do not communicate, they might get frustrated and ultimately this can play against you.

How Much Can It Pay?

If you are an employee you must be paid the minimum wage, which varies from one place to another. This information is easily accessible online. What you will earn will depend on your profile and experience but also on what is expected from you. Some parents may want you to do some cleaning for instance or to teach your native language to the kids if you speak a foreign language.

How to Find a Job in This Field?

Put the word out there that you are a babysitter and that you are looking for a job. The word of mouth works great in this industry. If there is a school in your neighborhood, see if there is a board where you could leave a small note with your contact information.

In parallel, advertise your services on internet. Creating an account is often free for babysitters, the parents are the ones usually paying the site, and it has become a significant share of the market so do not disregard your online presence. A word of advice here, be careful what picture you post on your profile as this will be the first impression you will make on the parents (your employers). A picture taken during your holidays in France is fine. A picture with your boyfriend, smoking a cigarette or posing as a model, not so much. Keep in mind that the parents are usually making a huge financial effort to pay you, and so they usually want a minimum of professionalism – and it helps build trust and confidence.

That being said, you can find countless offers on the following sites:

Bubble

www.joinbubble.com

Care

www.care.com

eNannySource

www.enannysource.com

SeekingSitters

www.seekingsitters.com

SensibleSitters

www.sensiblesitters.com

Sitter

www.sitter.com

Sittercity

www.sittercity.com

Sitting Around

www.sittingaround.com

UrbanSitter

www.urbansitter.com

28. Pet sitting

If you like pets, then pet sitting might be just right for you! Many pet owners do not have the time or the possibility to care themselves for their pets as much as they would like. Think about the professionals working for big firms in large cities who sometimes work 6 or 7 days a week, or who regularly finish working past 9:00 pm, not too say later. Think also about all the people who cannot leave their pets unattended, all by themselves, in their apartment for maybe as much as 10 hours, every day. And of course, you have the people leaving for a few days and who can't really take their pet with them. These are just a few examples. There is a huge market!

The first thing that comes to your mind is probably the pet owner who needs somebody to walk his dog. While this is a big part of the market, there is more to it and some owners need people like you to keep their animals all day, and this can pay very well.

Like for babysitters, you can work as an employee or have your own business. If you decide to be an independent contractor, make sure that you comply with all the applicable laws, including the possible need of a business license. You can most often find all the necessary information for free on the internet. Just make sure you do not forget anything, and in doubt make a call to the appropriate branch of the government.

One important aspect of this business is its legality. You must make sure that you are allowed to carry your activities where you live. For instance, if you live in an apartment, the number, size and type of animals that you can have with you might be regulated. In New York City, virtually every building has some sort of regulation regarding pets, which can go up to a clear and absolute prohibition. You do not want to violate the terms of your lease, or else.

Also, it's rather common for people engaged in this business to carry an insurance. Things can happen, and you want to be protected if a pet was to run away or if it was to die while in your custody. I am not trying to scare you here, but if you want to do things seriously you have to think like a professional and anticipate problems, even if they will likely never happen.

Common Requirements:

Education and skills: Anybody can become a pet sitter, as long as that person can in practice take care of a pet. Being an animal lover is a must as it will reflect directly on your work and your employers or clients will see it. If there is no specific level of education required, you might want to inquire about being certified by a professional organization.

See for instance:

Pet Sitters International

www.petsit.com

National Association of Professional Pet Sitters

www.petsitters.org

Equipment: It is recommended to have a computer with an internet access and a cell phone, but this is very basic equipment and most people already have that.

How Much Can It Pay?

You can usually expect to be paid between $12 and $25 per hour, but remember that you can take care of several animals at the same time.

How to Find a Job in This Field?

Like for babysitters you need to put the word out there in your neighborhood. See if you can place an ad at your local supermarket or other strategic places. In my neighborhood people use a forum called NextDoor (www.nextdoor.com). When I moved to my current address, I received a letter with an invitation to join a group created for my neighborhood on that site. I have to say that even if I do not use it often, I find it very valuable. I receive daily emails about things happening in my neighborhood, lists of people available for household work in the area, like babysitter and pet sitters. Check if this is available in your neighborhood as well or if there can be a similar service offered by another company. You can also start a group, if this is something you feel could gather interest where you live.

In addition, there is a number of websites that you can check to find work. See for instance:

DogVacay

www.dogvacay.com

Fetch! Pet Care, Inc.

www.fetchpetcare.com

Pet Sitters International

www.petsit.com

Rover

www.rover.com

Trusted House Sitters

www.trustedhousesitters.com/house-and-pet-

sitters

PetSitter.com

www.petsitter.com

29. Virtual Recruiter

Virtual recruiters are essentially salespersons specializing in finding the right employee for a specific position. They spend a lot of hours working from their computers, searching databases of resumes and social media sites, making phone calls and conducting interviews with potential job candidates to determine if they could be suitable for the position. Most of what recruiters do can be done remotely, not to say everything and, as a matter of fact, more and more companies rely on recruiters working out of the office. This is the same trend that we have been seeing for the past 15 years for legal and accounting jobs. Companies want to cut their costs and as a result outsource their work more and more often. In addition, the vast democratization of the technology has made this extremely easy: a good laptop can cost around $300.00 or so and sometimes less, high speed internet only costs about $50.00 per month and you can make national and international phone calls for close to nothing through Skype, a good cell phone costs about as much as your internet access, and you already pay for most of that anyway.

Companies can work with two types of virtual recruiters:

The first ones are employees working exclusively for them. They receive either a flat salary or a base salary with a commission based on their performance. Companies will often prefer experienced recruiters, even if their experience is rather short (a year or so sometimes). However, you can still find openings for complete beginners. A background in sales will also be an asset if you are new to recruiting.

The second ones are business people managing their own company and usually working for several clients. They have more freedom than the first ones and they are paid by commissions only when they place an employee. The commission is more important than in the first case but if they do not perform, they are not paid anything. If you decide to become your own boss, you can do this by starting from scratch from your house or apartment or you can join a program franchise to help you build your business, often specializing a field such medical, IT, compliance recruitment. The latter option is more expensive and won't work for many but if you can afford it, this can help you start your activity and receive the support and training you might need. However, you have never any guarantee that you will make a profit, so if you are interested in joining such a franchise or program, do your due diligence first by making sure that the business and claims are legitimate, and speak to other persons who have done it before you.

Common Requirements:

Education: Recruiters are not part of a regulated profession, so there is no minimum level of education that's absolutely required. Often, employers will prefer somebody who has at least a bachelor's degree, but this is just a trend, not an absolute rule or requirement.

English Language Skills: You must have excellent English language skills, grammar, and spelling. You are going to communicate with employers and if you can't express yourself correctly or write decent English this will directly impact your job performance. Your clients rely on you to present them serious and competent candidates. They might question your judgement if you can't write an email correctly. Being a recruiter is first and foremost a sales position and as such, presentation (even virtual presentation) is critical.

Knowledge & Professional Skills: You need to be comfortable using a computer and working with internet. You also need to be comfortable using a phone and making cold calls. All of that goes without saying. Now, having an understanding of the industry and of the job market in which you are going to operate is also key. Each profession has its own language and you must understand it a minimum. If you recruit lawyers or nurses for instance, you need to have a minimum understanding of what is going to be expected from the employee or you might lose your time or present candidates that are not fit for the position.

How Much Can It Pay?

If you work for a flat salary, you can expect to make between $19 and $30 per hour. If you are paid by commission, entirely or partially, then it will depend your performance. According to glassdoor.com, the average salary for virtual recruiters in the United States is a little under $50,000 per year

(www.glassdoor.com/Salaries/virtual-recruiter-salary-SRCH_KO0,17.htm).

How to Find a Job in This Field?

The websites listed in the introduction to this Chapter are the first places that you want to check. You should be able to find a good number of opportunities on them and recruiter is a job in demand. Do not limit yourself geographically. You can work for companies in other countries, provided foreign laws do not limit your ability to do so. If you choose to work as an independent contractor, you should not have any problem working remotely for a company located abroad. So do not hesitate to check out what other offers you can find elsewhere.

In addition to these sites, you can also take a look at the following job boards:

DaVita Medical Group

www.davitamedicalgroup.com

eZayo

www.ezayo.com/hr-jobs/9

HR Crossing

www.hrcrossing.com

HR Jobs

www.hrjobs.org

iHireHR

www.ihirehr.com

Michelle Stuhl & Company, Inc.

www.michellestuhl.com/contact/

(Send your resume to

resume@michellestuhl.com)

PeopleScout

www.peoplescout.com

Recruiting Jobs

www.recruitingjobs.com

Remote.co

www.remote.co/remote-jobs/recruiter/

30. Real Estate Investor Assistant & Wholesaler

If you are interested by real estate investments, or feel like you would be interested to learn how to become a real estate investor yourself, you might want to work as a Real Estate Investor Assistant. With the development of internet and of the resources available online you can now do so many things from the comfort of your own living room.

If you know where to look, you will find many real estate investors looking for sourcing assistants. As an assistant your job will mostly consist in finding good leads to investors. You will help investors by providing an address. You will also research the property in advance for things like existing liens, pending procedures against the owner or the property and so on. If you simply present random properties that you believe are interesting you will likely make little money, if any, and will eventually stop working in that field.

With the experience you will also be able to work as a real estate wholesaler, whether for residential or commercial properties. The work involved is very much the same but as a wholesaler you will have an interest in the property, a legal interest or an equitable interest, and this is this interest that you are going to sell to a real estate investor who can be for instance a contractor who will put the property in market condition before reselling it or an end buying.

Common Requirements

Education: Anybody can start working as a real estate investor assistant or as a wholesaler. There is no specific education or background needed. However, you are going to have to learn about real estate investing or to have to be trained by an experienced investor.

Professional Skills: You need to be able to make cold calls and be comfortable speaking to persons who can go through tough financial times.

Expenses: Some expenses are to expect but you can keep them usually low. Most information is available on internet for free. In some cases, you might have to pay to receive various lists from local governmental agencies or institutions. This usually does not go very far, a few dollars. Membership with a local real estate investor association is highly recommended. This can cost up to $400.00 usually, sometimes more. You may also have to send letters of flyers to a large number of real estate owner. Mailing a hundred flyers for instance is going to cost a little below $50.00, but it can cost more if you hire a third-party company to do it for you.

Equipment: You need a computer, a cell-phone and a connection to internet.

How Much Can It Pay?

Your income is going to depend on whether you can provide quality leads or assign rights to your investors. The sky is the limit as some would say, but in practice there is a learning period. Some can make a six-figure income regularly, others never make anything. What you will receive will be either a fixed amount or a percentage of the sale price. If you act as a wholesaler, you will assign your rights for the amount you and the investor will agree upon. It can be a few hundred dollars, it can be a few thousands.

How to Find a Job in This Field?

Here, you want to find investors. You are going to have to find them where they operate and meet: in the real estate section of an online advertisement websites and by attending real estate investment networking events. Craigslist is a good place to start.

You can check if there is a local chapter or group of the National Real Estate Investors Association in your area here: www.nationalreia.org/find-a-reia/. If not, you can still find other organizations and groups. There are plenty of them.

31. Host

If you own your main residence or if you rent and your lease agreement allows it, you might be able to rent a room or more to make some money. Many people are not necessarily interested in renting a full apartment or house. This is a fairly easy activity that only requires you to have a place to rent, to be legally allowed to conduct this activity where you live and to offer a decent and clean living space.

The downside of it is that you must select the persons staying at your place carefully. When you open your door to persons you do not know you may want to check who is going to share a living space with you. The money can be compelling argument but there are disrespectful people out there, and even some strange ones... If you have to share a common space, make sure that the rules are clear from day one.

You can also, if your property allows, open a bed and breakfast. For more on this you can check their requirements on the official website at www.bedandbreakfast.com/lyp.

Common Requirements

A Place You Can Legally Rent: If you rent your place, whether an apartment or a house, your lease might contain a provision against subleasing or against leasing all or part of the property. It's actually almost certain. There might also be some local regulations applicable in your area for this type of activity. Double check this with the city all, the county and the state. The best case scenario is when you own the property of course.

Treat Your Tenants the Best You Can: It does not mean you must accept anything or spend a lot of money to furnish a room. However, remember that today, on most websites, people can leave a comment about their stay and a bad review could affect your earning potential.

How much can I make?

It all depends on where you live. If you leave in NYC, in LA, or in Montreal, your earning potential can be great. If you live far from a big city, it will depend on your local real estate market and on the tourist attractiveness of the area.

Depending on where you live, this activity has the potential to bring you from a few hundred to a few thousand dollars every month.

How to Find Tenants?

You will find many websites where you can find people looking for a place to stay for a short stay or for a longer period. I would suggest that you focus on reputable websites, such as:

Airbnb

www.airbnb.com

BookaBach

www.bookabach.co.nz

EasyRoommate

www.easyroommate.com

HomeAway.com

www.vrbo.com

Naked Apartments

www.nakedapartments.com

OwnersDirect

www.ownersdirect.co.uk

SpareRoom.com

www.spareroom.com

VacationRentals.com

www.vacationrentals.com

32. Data Analytics and Data Analysis positions

The terms of data analytics and data analysis are often confused. Data analysis is a broader term that encompasses data analytics and data mining. Data analysis consists in compiling and analyzing data for business decision making purposes. Data analytics refers to the compilation of data using different tools and techniques.

Common Requirements

Education: Usually you will need to have a bachelor's degree (or more) in math, economics, statistics or computer science. A master's degree in data science will be an asset to gain employment or access to more advanced positions.

Skills: You will need to demonstrate advanced math, statistics and analysis skills and master Excel. It is also recommended to have programming skills and know basic SQL.

How Much Can It Pay?

These positions require advanced skills. Salaries start around $45,000 and go above $100,000.

How to Find a Job in This Field?

You can start your job search with the websites listed in the introduction of this chapter. You can complete your search with the following websites.

Anthem

www.antheminc.com

Freelancermap GmbH

(Some jobs for English speakers)

www.freelancermap.com

MoveOn Political Action

https://front.moveon.org/

If you have a background in mathematics, economics, statistics, computer science or finance and would like to explore further a career in this field, you can also check the following websites for more information:

TechAmerica

www.techamerica.org

Association for Computing Machinery

www.acm.org

33. Graphic Designer

Graphic designers are part artists part computer geeks. They design and implement graphic realizations for a variety of uses. They can work on the design of a company website, on the design aspect of various marketing products, work in the video game industry, in special effects for movies, for architects, in product development... They have a lot of options.

Common Requirements

Education: There is not one way to become a graphic designer, but many. Some attend university programs in various fields, some start as artists and transition to graphic design by learning on their own.

Computer Skills: You must definitely master Photoshop, InDesign, Illustrator and Dreamweaver. You should also be knowledgeable with html, CSS and Javascript.

Professional Skills: You must be an artist and you must be willing to learn constantly. Software and technics evolves all the time (think about 3D animations and virtual reality for instance).

How Much Can It Pay?

Graphic designers can work as independent contractors, running their own business. There is a huge depend for these skilled professionals. If this is the path they choose they can set their own fees. The more skilled and the more talented the more they can ask. Graphic designers can also work as employees. A beginner can expect to find a job from $15 to $25 depending on the job specifics and on the company, but salaries can go a lot higher.

How to Find a Job in This Field?

You can start your job search with the websites listed in the introduction of this chapter. They will provide a good number of resources. You can complete your search with the following websites.

Adhunter Ltd (adzuna)

www.adzuna.com/search?q=graphic%20web%2
odesigner%20remote&w=US

Authentic Jobs, Inc.

www.authenticjobs.com

Creativepool Ltd

www.creativepool.com

DesignCrowd

www.designcrowd.com

Dice

www.dice.com

Dribbbble

www.dribbble.com/jobs

OnPoint@Home

www.onpointathome.com/opportunities/

Stack Exchange Inc.

www.stackoverflow.com

WayUp, Inc.

www.wayup.com

Chapter 6: Make Money Selling on Amazon

The chances and opportunities available on Amazon are increasing day by day. Amazon has become a top player in the online shopping business. I am actually a big fan of Amazon and buy pretty much everything on this site. It has everything you can possibly think about and could need. Making online sales is a good method to make money working from home. There can be some (financial) risk involved, but not necessarily and not as important as one could think. Using drop shipping can indeed make online selling accessible to virtually everybody for very little. If paired with the correct methods and strategies, selling on Amazon can bring great opportunities for those who know how to find them.

Selling on internet is often considered as a method to generate a passive income. If you make the choice to sell online you will rapidly see that it can generate an active revenue. Sure, you only list your products once, but there is a lot more work to do after you sell, and if you do not do the work, you cannot earn a living.

In any event, do not disregard online retailing without giving it a thought, and Amazon has many great benefits to offer to beginners.

Amazon Allows You to Start Humble and Small

If you know anything about what goes into developing a website using e-commerce methods, you are already aware of the fact that it can be expensive and complicated at times. For people just beginning in this arena, diving head first into such a project might not be the smartest move.

Sure, it can work out, but what if it doesn't? Starting an e-commerce website project does not necessarily guarantee traffic online.

When you go with selling on Amazon, you benefit from all the work and all the investment amazon put into its website, and you would never be able to bring enough money and talent resources to achieve a result that could be even remotely close to what Amazon has to offer. With Amazon you can benefit from their existing global traffic and advanced sales and marketing methods. In addition, you can begin your selling journey even if you only have one product to sell. Then, you can work your way up, building your online business.

Many sellers fall in the trap of selling products for which there is no or too little demand. If you want to make money you need to go in a market where people are spending money. This does not mean that you should fall in the other trap: trying to sell what countless other people are already selling! This is the wrong way to go. Amazon will only display a certain number of seller per page for every product that is for sale, and they will appear by price. When you try to sell something that 40 other people are already offering you need to stand out of the crowd. If these people have bad reviews, this can be possible, otherwise you need to offer a different service such as international shipping or faster delivery, for instance by making clear where you are located (some buyers will prefer a seller located as close as possible in hope that this will result in a faster delivery). The other obvious way to differentiate yourself is to sell for the lowest price, but easier said than done and most people won't be able to do, at least at the beginning.

There are strategies and software out there to identify where there can be a market for you.

Amazon Allows You to Manage Your Time Efficiently

Selling on internet is often presented as a passive income way to earn money. I tend to disagree with that approach. It's only true to a certain extent. It takes a lot of work and in particular a lot of management, monitoring, and shipment work to make a living. Shipping and packing what you sell is quite straightforward and easy to visualize when you only have to send a couple of products per day, but what if you start selling more? What if you find yourself with over a hundred orders a day? This is time consuming. Although this sounds like the dream, it can be stressful when you take into consideration deadlines, shipments that cannot be delivered, and returns. If this looks like too much for you, you may wish to consider Amazon FBA, which stands for Fulfillment by Amazon.

Fulfillment by Amazon for Selling Online

How exactly does this differ from taking care of everything on your own? Here is an overview of the way it works.

First, you are going to ship your products in bulk to an Amazon warehouse. This usually requires that you already have a supplier. Here, instead of receiving the products at home, you are going to direct your supplier to send them all to an Amazon warehouse.

Amazon is going to store all your products for you and when you are going to make a sale, Amazon will take in charge the shipping of the product to your customer, so that you don't have to do it. It's a huge gain of time and a huge gain in efficiency. Most people selling this way never even see the products they sell.

Then, if there is a problem, Amazon will take care of returns and of customer service matters.

As you can see the advantages of using Amazon FBA are many, not to mention that Amazon operates 24/7 all year long and can even take care of international shipping. Plus, you get the full benefit of Amazon's great shipping options.

Selling using Amazon FBA program requires an upfront investment from the seller. You need to pay for your products (your inventory) before making the first sale. Sellers who want to start using this method can start for usually as little as $1,500 to $2,000, but it can go a lot higher. It's your job to know what risks you want to take and how much you know how much you can afford to put at risk. A number of sellers start with inexpensive items, costing usually below $10. That way they can order a few hundreds of them to get their business started.

Drop Shipping as an Alternative or as an Additional Method

If you cannot afford that type of investment or if you want to explore other methods at the same time, you might want to look into drop shipping. Drop shipping may be new to you but it has been around for many years. I was already using it about ten years ago. At the time, it wasn't a method that was as developed as it is today. Many suppliers where using that technique to get rid of products that were not always easy to sale. So, of course you were doing the heavy work sometimes with little results.

What is drop shipping?

Drop shipping is a sourcing method for online sellers allowing them to outsource most of the shipping workload and to minimize their financial exposure. When working with a drop shipping company you can list their products for sale online and not purchase any of them upfront. You will only pay for the products when, and only when, your clients buy them from you. When this happen, you will order the product from the drop shipper and it will then send it directly to your customer as if it was coming from you. Usually drop shipping companies do not take care of returns and do not handle customer service either. You will have to do it.

As you can see, drop shipping requires almost no investment from you to be in business.

Drop shipping as changed tremendously and you can now find great quality products to sale this way and the offer is now much more diversify than it used to be. That's definitely an option I would consider as a new seller.

If you want to learn more about drop shipping, I would recommend David Berman's book on

Passive Income, although again I disagree that it classifies as a passive income method. This author provides interesting practical information to get you started, including a great source to start your business today. Well worth the investment if you are a beginner.

Social Media

Social media platforms like YouTube, Twitter, and Facebook can help you share information about your business and products. If you already do this for fun and know a lot about it, that's a skill and strength you can bring to the table.

Sharing information with your existing Facebook friends is also quick and easy. You can list links to your products page. When you Tweet, you also increase your products' attention and the chance to close more sales.

A Blog Presence or Guest Blogging

Another way to get the word out there about your business is to publish on a personal blog or to write as a guest on somebody else's blog. Here you can share details about your products, share exciting information about your company, or even give out tips for people that are in a similar business, with links to your business page.

Diversification for Higher Chances of Success

There's no reason to depend entirely on just one platform for selling online. Some new online company owners think that they can only sell in one place, not on multiple websites, but that's not the case. There are a lot of plus sides to using more than one site. The more significant an audience you can share your product information with, the better. Don't decrease your chances of success by only sticking with one website. Try to sell on at least two, or ideally even more than that.

You Must Believe in Your Products

An important aspect to do business is to believe in your products. If you don't believe in your product, you will likely get bored and you will give up quickly. If you aren't into sports, don't sell memorabilia. If on the other hand, you're an artist, you might want to sell art supplies. You also need to understand the products because you will have to answer questions from potential clients. If what you're selling bores you, you can expect to be bored, and that's never good.

Chapter 7: Make Money

Selling on eBay

Everybody knows eBay, or at least have heard of it. It offers another great option to earn money while working from home. Unlike Amazon, eBay is known for being an auction website.

There are a few different types of auctions to be aware of as an eBay seller. Classic live auctions will allow you the highest amount of visibility. They typically work well for a broad audience and you can decide for how many days your auctions will run. Most buyers will first check out live listed items and a large number of people using this platform see bidding as a fun hobby. When you begin selling on eBay, opting for live auctions will allow you to be known as a company, and let people see that you exist.

Fixed-price listings, on the other hand, will allow buyers to see directly the price to pay for the item instead of waiting a few days. This usually covers a different market targeting people that don't have enough time to shop or wait around and who prefer to buy immediately. This can work well for you when you're just starting out because it allows you to get confident in your product because it's selling.

Here you can offer the possibility for the buyer to make a "best offer", meaning a lower offer than the price you ask. You can of course accept this counter-offer or reject it.

EBay also allows sellers to organize private auctions and auctions with a restricted access, something you probably do not want to try as a beginner who wants to generate quick and numerous sales.

Like when you start on Amazon, it's advisable to start simple and small. When you first start out, don't try to go big. Choose a product you're already knowledgeable about and can have a reasonably easy time selling. If you already have an idea, you're a step ahead. There's no reason to invent something new or share something that the world has never seen before. You can make money from common items such as coloring books. Also, check your competitors. It can give you precious indications about how products are selling and about other sellers' strategies.

Once you have found a product to sell and have determined that there can be a market to explore you have now to market your products.

Have an Easy Listing

You need to create a listing that's easy to navigate and catchy. Some sellers on eBay go over the top with their listing information and details, which can be overwhelming. Save your dreams of writing a novel for later and keep it simple and to the point.

You can just state what the item is, a small and accurate description, where you ship to, if the sale is final or if you accept refunds, and if your product is used or new. Then describe clearly the terms of shipping and in a perfect world a bit about how long it takes to arrive if you can figure out (this is a compelling argument for buyers).

Accuracy of Your Item Description

You need to describe what you're selling with accuracy and honesty. This includes the color, weight, size, and height of your item. Not everyone can tell these things from the picture, so remember that, and this can affect your reviews in a good or in a bad way. Inaccurate listings can kill your business before you even start it.

Pricing Information

Don't make the mistake of listing an item for less than you bought it for and assumed that people bidding on it will drive the price up, or if you do enter the minimum price at which the auction will become bidding.

Although some products on eBay don't sell successfully, there's no reason to drive down the price so far that you end up losing money. Remember that this process takes time. Don't list your product at a low price with the intention to save money on fees and charge high for shipping. This is by the way a practice prohibited by eBay.

If you cannot obtain a decent price for your product that covers all of your costs, including the value of the product, shipping and fees, you may want to rethink your sales and/or marketing strategy and eventually your market. Keep in mind that if your products don't sell on eBay, that isn't a sign that they are doomed to fail everywhere. Some products may sell fantastically on eBay, but not on other sites, and vice versa.

If you are motivated but are concerned about investing too much, I would invite you to go back to the section on drop shipping in the previous chapter. Drop shipping can help you start for cheap and test a market.

Visibility of Your Listings

On eBay you need to list your products under a certain category and you need to be as detailed as possible if you want to drive traffic to your products. The words you use are very important and you should think of them as key words triggering the public's attention. The idea is to make your title bring people to what you're selling, but there might be a learning curve to getting your products to show up in many different categories. Don't bother with paying extra to get your item listed in two categories. This not only makes you pay more, but it doesn't guarantee that you will make a sale. If you have something that someone wants, they are going to place a bid. Choosing the correct a good title enhances visibility at no additional cost.

Figure out Best Listening Times

Pay attention to when other people's auctions are coming to an end and find out whether there were bids on their products. When you decide to list your products outside of the time when your audience is present online, you lower your chances of making a sale. This will require some research on your part. All products will experience better deals during different times of day, depending on time zones.

Only Sell Authentic Items

You have to make sure that you aren't selling something that could come with issues of patent or copyright infringement. You must know where your product comes from and check it if you don't. Make sure you aren't violating any trademark laws either since you can get your store shut down by not paying attention to this.

The audience on eBay is worldwide, not just nationwide, so you will encounter problems by not adhering to these rules. It just isn't worth the hassle to lose your account when you can quickly follow the rules and enjoy success.

List Seasonal Items Early

If you're selling seasonal items, try to list them early, before the season hits. People look for deals outside of the high season since they know that prices will go up.

For instance, you can sell Easter products around Christmas time, since Christmas widens up the audience of shoppers on eBay. In fact, some shoppers only visit eBay around that time, so take advantage of that and list your items for other times of the year at that time.

Use Photos to your Advantage

When you take photos, remember that people are looking at your items on a flat surface (their computer screens), so people might have a hard time thinking about how that object really looks like. Have multiple photos of your item, and when appropriate place it next to other objects for size comparison. If you are selling clothes, try to take pictures of them hanging on a door, or better yet, on a mannequin. People want to know exactly what they're buying, so try to optimize visual aids.

If you find that your items aren't selling enough, remember that it's an ongoing learning process, and you will need some time to get people to buy from you. Buyers need to both like what you have to offer and to trust you as a seller.

People making money right away from selling the perfect product are an exception, and they are fortunate. Most sellers will need some time to figure out what works for them, to know how they should list their products, to fix fair prices, and to understand which products sell and which do not.

Save your Profits

There's a commonly accepted belief out there around running a business that you must re-invest everything you make in profits back into more products to sell. You don't need to do this since you want to generate earnings for yourself.

Instead, decide ahead of time what percentage of your profits you will re-invest into more merchandise. Don't learn the hard way and end up with more products than benefits. It can be tempting to become excited about your sales success and to over purchase.

Delivery Confirmations and Insurance

You need to use both on every item you sell. If a buyer claims that they never received a product, you need to have actual proof that it was sent out. Have principles on this and stick to them. For instance, if you decide that you are going to ship overseas, only do so using priority mail.

If someone asks you to ship it out at a cheaper rate, this could lead to the product taking a long time to arrive, and a customer leaving you a bad review because of that. Instead, do it in a way that is optimal for you and for the buyer.

Buying Clearance Items to Sell

One great way to get started, as a beginner online business owner, is to purchase items that are on sale in local stores. Keep in mind that there's always a risk involved with this since items on sale might be strange sizes or have some other quality defect that makes them less sellable.

These are all significant rules to observe as you're getting started with your eBay business. Let's look at some other factors to consider when you get into this field.

How to Handle Bad eBay Buyers

When you come across bad buyers on eBay, the best way to handle it is to simply block them to avoid selling to them again. Even if they leave you lousy feedback over something that is unfair, try to be the bigger person. At times, you might be tempted to warn other people by leaving them a wrong comment, but not commenting is simpler.

This shows that you are not the problem; the buyer is. Now, this can be much easier said than done, of course. Try working with people the best you can and use blocking as an absolute last resort. If you have a buyer that was very bad, you also have the option to report him to eBay.

If someone is causing problems with your store and leaving bad reviews or otherwise being difficult, they probably cause problems everywhere also. You cannot damage somebody's reputation and business unfairly. In this case do not hesitate to report that person.

Leaving negative feedback or replies to their negative comments might make you seem immature or unreliable. Merely block them, so they can't shop with you again. You can do this by visiting eBay's sitemap and clicking on block bidder, then typing in their username.

Which Layout Options Are Best For You?

Some people swear by trying to make the fanciest store page possible, to get a store on the web, and to invest in expensive graphics. Although this can be nice to try, if you can afford it, it does come out of your profits, if any. Otherwise you have to advance the funds. Remember that it's better to earn money before you go and spend it.

EBay provides free customizing options that won't cut into your profits. Stores that have nice logos and borders may attract more attention and more buyers, but it's not free and it has to be done right.

As a general rule, I would avoid the expense at the beginning and I would try to focus on making money come in. Ebay's template offer enough options and possibilities. Don't be afraid to play around until you find what works best for you and your personal needs. The advantage here is that eBay has made it simple to use and to understand, even if you are not a geek.

To summarize, start small, have your descriptions short and simple, have quality pictures, do not overspend and do not purchase too much inventory.

What If Your Idea Doesn't Work?

If you try this out and find that your original idea doesn't seem to earn you any money, you should diversify your sales through multiple platforms instead of just one, and you can always find other products to sell that work well.

Finally, Research Shipping Information

Shipping is relatively simple, but it never hurts to be over-prepared. When you start selling online, you have to be aware of what your costs are and you need to be able to explain all of that when you list your items. Buyers want to know. Once you figure out what factors are involved here, and help people understand that it cost money to ship to their house, you can start finding ways to save money on this.

The last place that I would recommend you check in this book is Shopify.

Chapter 8: Make Money
Selling on Shopify

I wanted to finish this book by mentioning another great website that you can use to make money from home: Shopify. This website is an excellent place to launch a business even if you have little money to invest into it. It can help you with running your store as a complete beginner.

What do People Sell on this Website?

If you are trying to sell physical items, use drop shipping, or sell a service or digital object (a legal one, of course), you can use Shopify to do it. When you visit this website, find out more by looking at the "E-commerce by Industry" section, where you will see a list of favorite items. Nearly anything you can think of can be sold on this platform. For those of you who have an existing retail or offline store, you can manage and merge your inventory and sales systems using Shopify.

How does Pricing Work on Shopify?

The flexible and varied pricing plans make Shopify a platform adapted for all types of businesses. Four main pricing plans exist, designed for improved functionality, extra tools and features to use for your e-commerce, and other items that can aid you in growing your online business.

There are no transaction or bandwidth fees when you process payments on Shopify, but the rates for credit cards will vary depending on the plan you choose.

They offer both paid and free options. Each plan option on Shopify is on a month to month basis, but you can also sign up for biennial or annual plans. You can cancel, downgrade, or upgrade all of this whenever you want to.

How Does Shopify Compare to Other Existing Options?

If you want to see how Shopify measures up to other platforms offering similar services, there's no need to create complicated charts for comparisons. Shopify has made this more comfortable for you. Figure out what past customers of previous websites and platforms think of the site, by searching through the section called "Comparisons" on the sitemap of Shopify.

There, you can read user testimonials from people who switched over to Shopify. These include comparisons with big-name sites such as Amazon and 3D Cart. One significant advantage of Shopify, as said before, is the ability to synchronize your offline and online sales with your physical stores. Rather than managing two separate systems, you can just use one.

How to Set Up Your Store Online with Shopify

You can choose to begin your store on a free two-week trial period that you receive when signing up. You will then enter your chosen store name, an email to use, and a password.

Choose a Simple Name

The name you choose for your store will be in the URL for your store. Although this can be changed later, if you wish, it's better to come up with something easy and simple now.

If you try to create a name that has many words, you will end up with something long and complicated. If you have plans for redirecting the URL from another site you have, like your main website or domain, you should keep your URL and store name in mind.

Enter your Information

As soon as you have your account created on Shopify, you will have to enter some necessary information, such as your phone number, address, and name. In addition to that, you will have to list what you're planning to sell and any current revenue you have. Then, you can create your store, using the following guidelines and tips.

Add in your Items

First, to set up your store, you need to add some items to sell. There are different guidelines for this depending on what you're selling.

Selling Physical Items

These should be entered manually, imported from other sites, like eBay, or uploaded in bulk from an existing CSV file.

Selling Digital Items

This requires you to install an online product delivery app, and add your items through that. To learn more about marketing digital issues, read the manual on Shopify's website.

Selling Services

If your store is intended for marketing services, use Product Options or another app that will let you choose custom settings and options. You are allowed to have a maximum of 100 different variations of each product in the store that goes under a few possibilities like finish, color, and size. These options are specific to each product, meaning that you can set individual options to one product, and different options to another.

Remember that options are not reserved for your physical products. You are free to use options in other ways, as well.

Instead of listing an e-book for sale and leaving it at that, for example, you could list a few different options for that book, including membership to your private forum, the e-book with extra material included, and lastly, just your digital edition. Visit Shopify to learn more information about this particular subject.

Your Store Design on Shopify

Your next step will be to add an exclusive design to the new store you've set up, which requires first that you choose a theme. You can find a great variety of themes in the theme store on Shopify, including both paid and free options categorized by specific industry.

If you haven't chosen to get a starter plan, edit the theme you picked by using the editor on the site. With most of the available topics, you'll want to visit these settings to add payment methods, social links, and other details to the footer.

The Domain Name on Shopify

If you want to customize your domain name, you can choose to do that at this stage. You can find more information on doing this in the online manual on Shopify, which provides all necessary documentation for setting it up. You can use your existing one or set one up on your own.

Taxes and Shipping

The next step will be to choose whether or not to add extra fees and shipping costs to your products, or telling Shopify that you already have them included in the price of your item. Shopify has already some necessary, simple rates to begin with. However, you might want to add some more choices and options, depending on the products you will be selling on your page.

Your Payments on Shopify

This is a crucial step: the way your customers will end up paying you for your services or products. For those of you in the United Kingdom, Canada, or United States, you can opt for accepting money using Shopify Payments.

This will allow your clients to use their credit cards, without the need of a third party to process them. In addition, Shopify provides options such as Google Wallet, Amazon Payments, and PayPal.

You must review the settings on your Shopify account very thoroughly. The majority of these points will already be filled in as you go through the steps listed above, but some details will have to be entered by you. These include your code for Google Analytics, the title of your store, and your store's description, and they can be adjusted in your general settings on Shopify.

Time to Open your Shopify Store!

As soon as you're prepared to do so, it's time to set your store to go public. Until the decision is made to do this, everything will be protected with a password, allowing you to test everything out to make sure it functions and looks how you want it to.

Just like with anything else, make sure you do plenty of testing so that you're the one who catches any glitches or mistakes, instead of your new customers. This may go without saying, but part of being professional as an online store is ensuring that everything is polished and ready to go.

Conclusion

I hope you find this book helpful and resourceful. With the many options you can choose from, tying yourself to a 9-5 job is no longer an option. The ideas we've discussed in this book are just the tip of the iceberg; if you do more research, you'll unearth many more active and passive incomes ways to make money from home.

My last piece of advice is very simple: keep your list of employers up to date and always keep looking for new employers or money making strategies as the market evolves all the time. Some source of income will appear, others will disappear. This will help you minimize your risks and maximize your earnings.

Finally, as a bonus for reading this book until the end, here is my last tip. Some companies will pay you to receive packages for your neighbors. Eneighbr for instance will pay you $3.50 per package just for opening your door. At the end of the week this can add up to a nice little amount. To learn more, you can check the company's website:

www.eneighbr.com/become_eneighbr.

Thank you again for purchasing this book!

If you have enjoyed this book, I would like to ask you if you would be kind enough to leave a review on Amazon. This may seem like nothing but it really does help to bring more great books.

Thank you again and good luck.

From the same author

Home *budgeting:* How to Manage Your Money, Stop Leaving from Paycheck to Paycheck and Get Out of Debt

Only on Amazon!

www.ingramcontent.com/pod-product-compliance
Lightning Source LLC
Chambersburg PA
CBHW071118050326
40690CB00008B/1260